Victoria

THE ESSENTIAL

TEA

COMPANION

Victoria

THE ESSENTIAL TEA COMPANION

*Favorite Recipes for
Tea Parties and Celebrations*

HEARST BOOKS

New York

HEARST BOOKS
New York

An Imprint of Sterling Publishing
387 Park Avenue South
New York, NY 10016

Portions of this book have previously appeared in the following titles:
The Charms of Tea, The Pleasures of Tea, and *The Art of Taking Tea*

Project Editor: Sarah Scheffel

Designer: Alexandra Maldonado

Contributors: Kim Waller, Mary Goodbody, Linda Sunshine, Catherine Revland, and Sarah Scheffel

This book was previously published as a hardcover.

ISBN 978-1-61837-134-8

Distributed in Canada by Sterling Publishing
c/o Canadian Manda Group, 165 Dufferin Street
Toronto, Ontario, Canada M6K 3H6

Distributed in the United Kingdom by GMC Distribution Services
Castle Place, 166 High Street, Lewes, East Sussex, England BN7 1XU

Distributed in Australia by Capricorn Link (Australia) Pty. Ltd.
P.O. Box 704, Windsor, NSW 2756, Australia

For information about custom editions, special sales, and premium and corporate purchases,
please contact Sterling Special Sales at 800-805-5489 or specialsales@sterlingpublishing.com.

Manufactured in China

2 4 6 8 10 9 7 5 3 1

www.sterlingpublishing.com

To tea lovers everywhere:

*We hope you will
make a little time to
indulge in the pleasures
of tea everyday.*

Contents

Tea and Special Occasions • 81

Indulge in our favorite menus for tea parties and celebrations

More Delightful Recipes for Teas and Treats • 117

Delight friends and family with our teatime recipes, from home-brewed teas to delectable sweets and savories

Resources • 183

Introduction

Whenever the fragrance rises from a fresh-poured cup of tea, a sense of comfort, peace, and ceremony accompanies it. Perhaps that's why, in most of the world, the taking and offering of tea signifies trust and friendship. It's an occasion, a moment of calm to which the harsher realities are simply not invited. In fact, ever since this beguiling beverage from China was introduced to Holland and England, teatime has been a social and civilizing event, a chance to deepen old friendships and develop new ones.

We invite you to take part in this time-honored tradition by offering you ideas and inspiration for a joyous range of tea parties, from special-occasion teas (think holiday housewarmings and bridal showers) to a spur-of-the-moment picnic or relaxing late-afternoon cup with friends. Our advice on must-have china and chintz, as well as our overview of silver tea accessories and traditions, will help make you a confident hostess. And then there are the recipes: More than a hundred irresistible teas, sandwiches, breads, and spreads, not to mention cookies, cakes, and tarts you can mix and match at your next celebratory tea.

Whatever the occasion, giving a tea party allows you the opportunity to entertain good friends and kind acquaintances with sweet style. Take care with the food, brew a bracing pot of tea, but most important, enjoy the warmth and joy possible only when good friends gather for a party.

Opposite: Creamware and gleaming silver—a happy English marriage that has lasted since the eighteenth century.

Getting *Acquainted* with *Tea*

Could there be anything more elemental than a cup of tea? Yet in its clear depths lies a great saga of East and West, of ceremony and enterprise. "Its liquor is like the sweetest dew of heaven," wrote Lu Yu, tea's first scholar-poet, circa 750 A.D. Even then tea was valued in China, its land of origin, for those medicinal qualities we are only now able to document. But tea does more than brace the body, said Lu Yu; it opens the eye of the spirit, it suffuses one with peace.

Opposite: A woven tray makes tea-time perfectly portable.

With each sip I taste
The fire that gives its heat,
The water that gives its wetness,
The leaf that gives its spell.

—The Minister of Leaves

For the Love of Tea

After Lu Yu's influential book, *Ch'a Ching*, or "Classic of Tea,"
was published, nine hundred years would pass before European
sea traders imported tea to Holland, and from there to England.
Suddenly, the exotic elixir of China was all the rage among
stylish folk.

In seventeenth-century Holland, guests at grand tea
parties drank as many as fifty small cups with rich cakes,
followed by brandy and raisins. At the English court, King
Charles II's queen, the Portuguese Catherine de Braganza,
popularized tea. The fashion filtered from coffeehouse to
manor house, "sheering the whole land from the palace to
the cottage," as one observer put it. Initially tea was so pre-
cious that it was locked away in strongboxes. Demand for

Above: A globe-bedecked
teapot serves as a reminder of
how far tea travels before it ends
up brewed in your cup.

Opposite: Porcelain, in
this case of new manufacture,
ensures purity of taste for even
the subtlest teas.

15

this and other profitable luxuries of the East, including silk and porcelain, launched the powerful British East India Company on the high seas to Canton. The China trade eventually started England on a tea-drinking way of life, forever replacing ale as the national breakfast drink. By the 1750s, Samuel Johnson, for one, had become such a "hardened and shameless tea-drinker" that he swore his kettle barely ever cooled.

❧ Left: Tea has its myths, and so do tea cups: On Wedgwood jasperware, goddesses frolic.

❧ Opposite: Tea has always offered a convenient excuse for collecting accoutrements, such as this lustrous china.

A World of Customs

Perhaps we'd be surprised to see well-dressed guests slurping tea from their saucers, but that was once the custom in England and America. Certainly, the habit cooled the steaming beverage a bit.

Long before the West made a social event of tea, however, Zen Buddhist monks brought the leaf from China to Japan, where in 1588 the tea master Rikyu formalized a poetic ritual still practiced today, a ceremony requiring a slower arrangement, and the beauty of the tea utensils. In the relationship of host to guests, of each object to another, students of the Japanese tea ceremony find a calm beyond the ruckus of the everyday world.

16

If man has no tea in him, he is incapable of understanding truth and beauty.

—Japanese proverb

A Miraculous Plant

Many of us rely on the convenience of a tea bag. We dunk it a few times, then discard it. Perked with lemon or milk, perhaps a bit of sugar, our cuppa, as the British say, is just fine. Familiar. Handy. Hot.

Imagine, now, a terraced hillside, green and misty, in India or Taiwan. Between curving rows of chest-high tea plants, shawled women move slowly, pinching off only the youngest leaves, perhaps some with tender buds.

If the tea plant, *Camillia sinensis*, were left alone, it would grow into a wild, sturdy tree thirty-five feet tall. But in the long-cultivated tea gardens of the East, it is tended as carefully as the grapevines of Champagne—and harvested far more frequently.

Above: We may think of teatime as a British tradition, but the motifs on this blue willow china remind us of tea's Eastern origins.

Opposite: To those who truly love them, teas are as deliciously subtle as wines.

This one miraculous plant (with many sub-varieties) gives us an amazing range of subtle brews. Soil, climate, and elevation, regular or unexpected weather conditions—all affect flavor. But most important, the method of curing the leaves determines which of these basic styles of tea you will drink: green, oolong, or black.

Once picked, all tea leaves are dried enough to eliminate moisture and start the process of oxidizing, a chemical change known—misleadingly—as fermentation. For delicate green tea (the favorite in China), that process is very quickly arrested by firing, or heating. Heartier black tea (the favorite in the West) is fermented much longer. Oolong falls between, in both processing and flavor. Rolling and bruising the leaves to release the juices is important, too, and may be done several times between repeated firings until the leaves are finally crisp and dry. Traditionally, all this was accomplished by hand (and sometimes foot); today, in major tea gardens, machines and ovens have taken over.

✏ Opposite: To replicate the mood of an Asian tea salon at home, serve sencha (Japan's favorite green tea) in small ceramic cups without handles. A woven tray and spare flower arrangement complete the mood.

✏ Below: A rose-patterned tea set lends any gathering the mood of a garden party.

"China or India?"

Thus did hostesses once inquire about one's preference, meaning, basically: green or black?

China tea, including the long-popular scented jasmine, has the reputation of being a meditative sip, while India tea is considered bracing. But so considerable are the differences among the teas of India alone, the world's largest producer, that saying "India" to a tea connoisseur is like saying "blue" to Rembrandt. And what of Japan, Formosa, Taiwan, Sri Lanka? They, too, produce lovely teas worth knowing. As for the supermarket tea bag, its contents probably come from Australia, where the leaves are harvested by machine.

A MIRACULOUS PLANT

Putting a Formal Shine on Teatime

There is something about the very essence of tea that suggests a bit of ceremony in the serving. For eighteenth-century aristocrats, as for proper Victorians, a full silver tea service on its tray, or salver, flashed a beautiful message of hospitality—with entirely intentional overtones of status and prosperity. Silversmiths lavished their artistry on every element of the tea equipage, and for generations the silver tea set was among the proudest of heirlooms. But after World War II, all that polishing and propriety seemed just too much bother. The result is that fine silver tea implements became widely available for collectors with a gleam in their eye. They remain so today.

Above: Any tea tastes special when served in dainty china cups.

Opposite: Whether it's a family heirloom or thrift shop find, a full silver tea service puts the "high" in "high tea."

Teatime Essentials

Aside from the usual teapot, hot water urn, and coffeepot, here are some other pieces to collect. For a more comprehensive list of tea equipment, see page 186.

CREAMER AND SUGAR BOWL
This most useful duo will always shine at dinner parties and family gatherings.

STRAINER
Place over the cup to catch loose tea leaves as you pour from the pot. Or use it to strain the seeds from squeezed lemons.

SUGAR TONGS AND LEMON FORKS
They're showy yet delicate. Use them as helpers on an hors d'oeuvres tray.

TEA CADDIES
Of course, these would be lovely on the vanity. Better yet, preserve your prize first-flush Darjeeling in style.

TEASPOONS
Hunt for your engraved first or last initial in antiques shops.

Clockwise from right: A full silver service on a tray; a whimsical silver pot and creamer; and a make-shift sugar bowl paired with an engraved teaspoon. For an elegant example of a tea strainer, see the photo on page 22.

Opposite: China teacups and saucers are teatime essentials, too. Here scalloped cups and saucers are prettily mismatched with serving pieces in a complimentary floral pattern.

24

Tea is nought but this:
First you heat the water,
Then you make the tea.
Then you drink it properly.
That is all you need to know.

—Sen Rikyu, Zen tea master

Must-Have China

If you are sailing from China to England with silk and tea on board, the last thing you want to do is get the cargo wet. Water ruins both products, so they were carried in the middle of the ship. Fortunately, the perfect ballast to stack in the hold in the 1700s was exactly what all of Europe and the American colonies were clamoring for: Chinese porcelain. Although many Western attempts were made to approximate its fine hardness (based on a clay called kaolin that withstood high-temperature firing), none really succeeded. People bought porcelain off the ships or placed orders with the Chinese potters of Jindezhen to create a full set, perhaps adorned with the family crest, and well worth waiting for.

Above and opposite: When kaolin, the fine white clay from which porcelain is made, was discovered in Europe in the late 1700s, a golden age of porcelain was launched.

Such was the rage for "china" in England that it was soon being displayed "on every chimney-piece, to the tops of ceilings, until it became a grievance," carped Daniel Defoe. (Proudly displayed china is still a stalwart of English decorating.) Thought fools for beautiful china, those early collectors were hardly foolish: Glorious handpainted Chinese export wares are highly valued today by museums. (One of the very best collections can be seen at the Peabody Museum in Salem, Massachusetts.) To this day, no substance is kinder to tea than hard paste porcelain, which imparts no flavor of its own.

The Lure of Blue Willow

Blue willow is the most popular china pattern ever known, made in many hundreds of versions for hundreds of years. At first, English potters copied Chinese design elements—here a pagoda, there a bridge—on their affordable earthenware. Sometime in the late 1700s, the willow pattern we know and love was born in the factories of Stoke-on-Trent.

The best-known tale inspired by the pattern first appeared in an English magazine in 1849. It tells of a well-born maiden, Koong Shee, in love with Chang, a lowly secretary. Forbidding her to marry beneath her station, her father, a wealthy mandarin, locks her up until her arranged wedding to another. But the lovers escape with the help of a gardener, racing over a bridge to hide on the island. They are found by the furious father. As his murderous wrath descends upon the lovers, the merciful gods transform them into doves, eternally paired in flight. "I wouldn't be one to deny it," wrote an anonymous poet, "For the little blue dove and her mate / Forever flying together/Across my Willowware plate."

The Timelessness of Wedgwood

If your antique teacup is stamped "England" on the bottom and not "Made in England," its date is before 1908.

And if it is also stamped "Wedgwood," you hold in your hands a work of one of England's longest-thriving pottery firms, whose wares have been prized since the 1770s. Its founder, Josiah Wedgwood I, worked years to perfect Jasper, right, adorned with delicate, cameo-like figures from classical mythology, and still the most recognizable of Wedgwood's many creations. His lovely creamware (called "Queen's ware" after Queen Charlotte acquired a tea set in 1765) graced tables throughout Europe and America. Today, brides can pick from elegant patterns, new and historic, each piece proudly stamped "Wedgwood."

Other Uses for Tea

TEA-DYE linen fabrics or tired-looking white cottons and prints: blouses, drapes, nightgowns. A mixture of black tea and plum tea gives a soft pinkish cast.

CREATE "antique" documents or a treasure-hunt map. Roughly tear the edges of a firm white paper, crinkle it up, then spread it out. Run a hot tea bag over the paper, blotching it here and there. If the look is not aged enough, let the paper dry, then blotch again.

SOOTHE sunburn or bee stings with a chilled used tea bag or used leaves. This is also an excellent poultice for puffy or tired eyes.

FOR A FACIAL, put plenty of chamomile tea and hot water in a large bowl. When the steam is safe, bend over the bowl, your head tented by a towel, and feel the steam open your pores.

GIVE YOUR PLANTS A BOOST by treating them to your leftover tea. Mix used leaves (not the bag) into houseplant or garden soil. Roses love it!

❧ Opposite: Match teacups and saucers in form or spirit, if not in pattern. Collecting odd ones is more fun if you look for one color or a particular maker.

Tea set:
6 cups.
saucers and
plates.   £55.

Bathroom
cabinet
£62.00

We always had our tea out of those blue cups when I was a little girl, sometimes in the queerest lodgings, and sometimes on a trunk in the theater.

—Willa Cather, *Alexander's Bridge*

The Collector's Cup

What turns a drink of tea into an occasion? Often, the cup it is served in—no doubt one reason why so many tea lovers are just as devoted to lovely china as they are to their orange pekoe or lapsang souchong. However, your tea set doesn't need to be Wedgwood or blue willow to bring joy and beauty to teatime. In fact, your tea set doesn't even need to be a proper set. Collecting can start with the jog of a childhood memory—perhaps a swirl of rosebuds recalls some long-ago cup in which an adored grandmother offered you a bit of sweet, milky tea scented with cinnamon. Soon you're haunting flea markets or scanning the shelves of antiques shops for others of its style or pattern—or mixing and matching patterns in a way that pleases you.

There are many individual ways to build a collection you'll love to display, use, and share with friends. One casual collector never passes up a nice teacup patterned with pansies, new or old (or an embroidered napkin for that matter).

Above and opposite: Antique, vintage, or new, a rose-patterned tea set is sure to charm.

Another has not only become an expert on blue-and-white English transferware from 1790 to 1830, but has styled her dining room—from wallpaper to needlepoint chair seats—to complement her collection. Since teacups (especially the handles) are perilously fragile, some we discover are orphans, perhaps survivors of a fine set of Meissen or Sèvres made long ago. Let fancy be your guide, then, and pick only the prettiest for a mixed collection in which each cup is a dazzling individual.

♪➤ Left and right: Charming vintage cups are perfect for everyday tea, while delicate scalloped teacups bring luster to formal occasions.

And if one day you find yourself in yet another cluttered little shop, turning over a saucer to study the maker's mark, running a finger around the rim to check for nicks, holding a cup to the light to detect repairs, you'll know it for sure: You've become a collector.

Clockwise from top left: Irresistible tea cups, including four teacups from Limoge, "A la Reine" at front; "Lotus" teacup from Mikasa; "Lady Carlyle" teacup from Royal Doulton; "Samoa" teacup from Jean Louis Coquet.

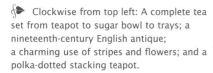 Clockwise from top left: A complete tea set from teapot to sugar bowl to trays; a nineteenth-century English antique; a charming use of stripes and flowers; and a polka-dotted stacking teapot.

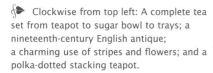 Opposite: A tea lover proudly displays a handsome collection of teapots.

36

The Charm of Chintz

As crowded with blossoms as an English cottage garden, chintzware, in myriad bygone patterns, is sought avidly by those who fall under its innocent spell. Despite today's climbing prices, this was once humble daily china, a blithe flower show that brightened ordinary English homes and was just as cheerful as the fabric it was derived from. Indeed, the story is told of chintzware's originator, Leonard Grimwade, founder of the Royal Winton potteries in Stoke-on-Trent, that he once stopped a lady in the street so he could copy the floral pattern of her pinafore. In the heyday of chintzware—the 1920s to the 1960s—many potteries were turning out patterns with fetching names like "Julia," "Sunshine," "Hazel," and "Summertime," each a favorite of collectors today.

Above and opposite: Very little chintzware was made after the 1960s, so a complete "Summertime" tea set with its own tray is a rare find. Many collectors simply mix and merrily unmatch.

39

Above and opposite: Intriguing shapes such as the square "Julia" sugar bowl, above, and overall patterns like those in the "Summertime" set, opposite, are part of chintzware's appeal. Paper patterns (which grew brighter after the 1940s) were applied to the china by hand.

You can never get a cup of tea large enough or a book long enough to suit me.

—C.S. Lewis

Living with Tea

Tea is such a pleasant part of our lives that its accoutrements have a sly way of escaping the table to join the general décor. Indeed, the mere fact that we might have a round, pedestal tea table anchoring a bouquet of tea roses (named for their evocatively similar scent), and that we set our table and measure our cooking ingredients with teaspoons are proof positive that tea has long been at home with us. But why stop there? Enlisting a favorite teapot or creamer to hold a clutch of wildflowers is only a beginning. One collector found herself selecting fabrics and rugs that played happily into the mood of her tea sets. Another tea lover ornaments her dining room sideboard with a handsome Russian samovar; still another hangs her grandmother's perforated silver tea balls (once used to steep loose tea in a cup) on the Christmas tree—as gleaming family ornaments.

Above and opposite: Creating a space to enjoy your morning cup is one joy of collecting. A decorating scheme that blends casual comfort with evocations of the past lends itself well to a display of tea things, as cheerful to look at as they are to use. A cup given by a friend or a row of ceramic pots gathered on one's travels speak always of hospitality.

43

He brewed his tea in a blue china pot, poured it into a chipped white cup with forget-me-nots on the handles, and dropped in a dollop of honey and cream. "I am," he sighed deeply, "contented as a clam."

—Ethel Pochocki, *Wildflower Tea*

The kitchen is tea's cheerful home ground, a good place for a bit of whimsy in the wallpaper or a show of colorful crockery. If the tea blends you collect start to overflow their cabinet, why not dedicate an open shelf to them, all fresh in rows of the old-fashioned labeled tins with tight lids called caddies. Then whatever your mood, you'll be able to reach for the right tea.

One particularly useful invention, the table whose tray top is detachable, makes it easy to carry tea things (or cocktails or canapés) in from the kitchen without having to clear a surface to set them on. When not a tray, it's a table; perfect for a smaller house.

❧ Opposite: It's possible to have your cup and delightful café curtains, too. A lighthearted touch brings teacups to printed upholstery cottons and pillow shams. If blue-and-white Staffordshire is your cup of tea, why not flaunt your passion on a wallpaper border, stencil, needlepoint pillow—even stationery—as well?

Making *Time* for *Tea*

Tea is a daily companion that never fails us. It warms when we—or the world—feel cold, gives strength when we're weary, and lends delicious grace notes to our gatherings. From the first cheery chortle of the kettle at dawn to the fragrance of an evening cup as the house quiets and we turn to our reading, tea can be counted on to smooth and save the day.

Opposite: A pretty tea set makes teatime special, whether you're enjoying tea with a friend or solo.

Morning's First Cup

Brew a cup; brew a day. Unhurriedly. The sunrise song of tea is lyrical, but with bracing undertones. "Of course you can," it murmurs encouragingly. The flavor holds a hint of far lands, yet is as familiar as the cat that comes to nuzzle your leg or sunlight on the windowsill. And as you lift your first cup of tea and feel its warmth, the day's challenges settle into perspective. A breakfast tea implies breakfast—an important meal we're often tempted to skimp on or rush through. But those hearty, homey smells of breakfast filling the kitchen are part of morning's joy and childhood's memories, whether it's homemade English muffins to slather with jam or simply a bit of sugared cinnamon gilding the toast. When you take the time to fortify yourself or your family with something special like blueberry fritters, you are making a sovereign statement: This part of the day is about us.

Above: A cup of tea and a slice of buttered toast are a pleasant start to any morning.

Opposite: Can every day hold a bit of Sunday? Not always, but when you or a loved one are about to depart on a trip (or have just returned from one), a tasty breakfast with tea beautifully served at bedside restores both body and spirit.

49

Breakfast in Bed

It needn't be an anniversary or a birthday for you and your beloved to indulge yourselves with a lavish breakfast in bed. What a cozy way to celebrate being together again after a business trip, or simply to say on any Sunday, "We're special, we deserve it." Turn off the phone, spread the newspaper all over the bed if you like, and read the best bits aloud to each other. Make a pact: No weighty discussions about children or finances allowed.

Let the tray you present be just as special. Line it with one or two of your finest linen napkins—to soften the clinks and clangs—then "set the table" with the best silver pot and porcelain cups to fill with bracing Earl Grey or English breakfast tea. Add buttered crumpets and jam and perhaps several hard-boiled eggs, and this infrequent treat could easily become a new weekend ritual.

To emphasize this point, indulge the eye as well as the taste buds. A bedside repast with fresh flowers on a lace-lined tray (and never mind the inevitable crumbs on the quilt) is not for newlyweds alone: Try it midlife, before the most stressful of working days.

For some people, starting the day means wrapping hands around a favorite sturdy mug; others see no reason to reserve the beauty of an antique cup just for guests. Whichever you might choose, there's a ritualistic comfort in using pretty objects you love that no impersonal carton from the corner deli can impart. (Moreover, cardboard and Styrofoam are inimical to tea's subtle flavors.)

As you infuse your morning with the invigorating aroma of tea, you are taking a brief, quiet stand against the utilitarian world. These moments belong to serenity.

Above: Tea blends with hearty wakeup notes, such as English and Irish breakfast teas, lend courage to the morning. Usually a mix of Ceylon and Assam, often with Darjeeling, these teas stand up well to a splash of milk.

Opposite: Breakfast in bed, complete with a teacup full of flowers, is the perfect indulgence for you and your partner.

50

Orange pekoe tea, a flowery, favorite morning blend, has nothing to do with oranges. To impart elegance, Dutch traders named this tea for the princes of the House of Orange; today it refers to the size of the leaf picked.

English Muffins

English muffin purists insist that you should never slice open a muffin to toast it. Instead, cut a sliver in the side and toast it whole. When done, poke butter in through the slit and savor the muffin with your morning cup.

Makes 10 to 12 muffins

¼ cup warm (110°F) water

Pinch of sugar

1 envelope active dry yeast

1½ cups warm (110°F) milk

2 tablespoons unsalted butter, cut into bits and softened

1 tablespoon honey

About 5¼ cups all-purpose flour

1¼ teaspoons salt

Cornmeal

1. In a small bowl, combine the warm water and sugar. Sprinkle the yeast over the top and let stand until the yeast dissolves and becomes foamy, about 10 minutes.

2. Meanwhile, butter the large bowl of an electric mixer. Combine the milk, butter, and honey in the bowl and stir until the butter is almost melted.

3. Stir in 2½ cups flour and the yeast mixture. Beat at high speed for 3 minutes, or until well combined. Cover the dough with a tea towel and let it rise in a warm place, away from drafts, until it is doubled in volume, about 30 minutes.

4. Butter a 4-quart mixing bowl and set aside. Stir the salt into the dough. With a wooden spoon, stir in enough of the remaining flour so the dough forms a ball.

5. Turn the dough out onto a well-floured surface. Knead the dough until it is smooth and elastic, about 8 to 10 minutes, adding enough of the remaining flour to keep the dough from sticking. Transfer the dough to the prepared bowl, turning it once to coat the top of the dough with butter.

6. Cover the dough with a tea towel and let it rest in a warm place, away from drafts, until it is doubled in volume, about 45 minutes.

7. Punch the dough down and divide it in half. Sprinkle a bread board generously with the cornmeal. Place half the dough on the board and sprinkle more cornmeal over the top of the dough.

8. Gently roll the dough out into a ½-inch-thick round. Cut out the English muffins with a floured 3-inch biscuit cutter. Repeat with the remaining dough. Arrange the dough rounds 2 inches apart on ungreased baking sheets. Knead, reroll, and cut the dough scraps once, if desired.

9. Cover the muffins with a tea towel and let them rise in a warm place, away from drafts, until they are doubled in volume, about 30 minutes.

10. Heat a lightly oiled nonstick griddle or skillet over medium-high heat. Lift some of the dough rounds with a spatula onto the griddle. Cook for 2 minutes on each side, then reduce heat to medium and cook, turning every few minutes, for 13 to 18 minutes, until done in the center.

11. Cool the muffins on wire racks while you cook the remaining muffins.

Strawberry–Lemon Balm Butter

Delightful with homemade English muffins, this special butter perks up even ordinary toast and pancakes. It's a perfect recipe for kitchen gardeners: lemon balm and strawberries are both ready for picking in June.

Makes about 1 1/3 cups

1 cup (2 sticks) softened
unsalted butter

3 tablespoons confectioners' sugar
or more to taste

1/3 cup finely chopped strawberries

2 tablespoons chopped
fresh lemon balm

1. In a food processor, combine the butter and confectioners' sugar. Process until the mixture is creamy.

2. Add the strawberries and lemon balm. Pulse just until the mixture is well combines. (If the strawberries are particularly tart, add another table of confectioners' sugar.)

3. Transfer the butter to a small bowl, cover with plastic wrap, and refrigerate until ready to serve.

Right: When it's time to cook English muffins, invite your "assistant chef" to lend a hand.

Spicy Rose Tea

If you don't have pesticide-free rose petals handy, substitute pesticide-free lavender flowers, borage flowers, or sweet violets for an equally fragrant, eye-opening blend.

Makes 4 to 6 servings

1 tablespoon fresh pesticide-free
rose petals or 1 teaspoon dried

4 teaspoons orange pekoe tea

1/2 teaspoon cinnamon stick chips

1. Pour boiling water into the teapot and set aside for 5 minutes. Discard the water.

2. Gently crush the rose petals to release their flavor. Put them into a tea ball along with the tea and cinnamon chips. Cover the tea ball and place in the teapot. Cover with boiling water and steep for 5 minutes.

3. Remove the tea ball from the teapot and discard the solids. Serve the tea immediately.

Cinnamon-Raisin Bread

For an intriguing twist on this swirly bread, soak the raisins in black tea, then drain well before adding them to the batter. When choosing foods for a breakfast menu, bear in mind that anything with spice stands up to robust black teas like Ceylon, orange pekoe, and Darjeeling.

Makes 2 loaves

Raisin Dough

1/4 cup warm (110°F) water

3 tablespoons sugar, plus a pinch

1 envelope active dry yeast

3 tablespoons unsalted butter, cut into bits

1 1/2 teaspoons salt

2 cups warm (110°F) milk

6 1/2 to 7 cups all-purpose flour

1/2 cup dark raisins

1/2 cup golden raisins

Cinnamon Filling

1/2 cup sugar

1 tablespoon ground cinnamon

TO MAKE THE RAISIN DOUGH

1. Butter two 9- by 5- by 3-inch loaf pans. Butter a 4-quart bowl. Set aside.

2. In a small bowl, combine the warm water and the pinch of sugar. Sprinkle the yeast over the top and let stand until the yeast dissolves and becomes foamy, about 10 minutes.

3. Meanwhile, in the large bowl of an electric mixer, combine the remaining 3 tablespoons sugar, the butter and salt. Pour in the warm milk. Stir until the butter is almost melted.

4. Stir in 3 cups flour and the yeast mixture. Beat at high speed for 3 minutes. With a wooden spoon, stir in the raisins, then stir in enough of the remaining flour so the dough forms a ball.

5. Turn the dough out onto a well-floured surface, and knead the dough until it is smooth and elastic, 8 to 10 minutes, adding enough of the remaining flour to keep the dough from sticking. Place the dough in the prepared bowl, turning it once to coat the top of the dough with butter.

6. Cover the dough with a tea towel and let it rise in a warm place, away from drafts, until it is doubled in volume, 1 1/4 to 1 1/2 hours.

7. Punch the dough down. Turn it out onto a well-floured surface, and divide it in half. Cover the dough with a tea towel and let it rest for about 10 minutes.

TO MAKE THE CINNAMON FILLING

8. Meanwhile, in a small bowl, combine the sugar and cinnamon.

9. Roll half the dough into a 12- by 8-inch rectangle. Sprinkle with half the cinnamon filling. Press the filling into the dough.

10. Starting at the short side, roll the dough up tightly, jelly-roll fashion. Pinch the dough together at the seam. Pinch the ends to seal and fold under the loaf. Place seam side down in a prepared loaf pan. Repeat with the remaining dough.

11. Cover the dough with a tea towel and let it rise in a warm place, away from drafts, until it is doubled in volume, 45 to 60 minutes.

12. Preheat the oven to 375°F.

13. Bake the loaves for 40 to 45 minutes. Tent the pans loosely with aluminum foil during the last 15 minutes to prevent over-browning.

14. Remove the loaves from the pans and cool slightly on wire racks.

Blueberry Fritters

These crisp fritters must be served as soon as they are cooked. The temperature of the frying oil is crucial, so be sure to allow it to reheat between batches.

Makes 10 to 12 fritters

Oil, for deep-frying

1 cup all-purpose flour

¼ cup granulated sugar

1¼ teaspoons baking powder

½ teaspoon salt

¼ teaspoon ground cinnamon

¼ teaspoon ground nutmeg

¼ teaspoon ground allspice

2 large eggs, separated

1 tablespoon fresh lemon juice

1 teaspoon vegetable oil

⅓ cup milk

½ cup dried blueberries

Confectioners' sugar for garnish

1. In a deep fryer, heat the oil to 375°F. In a medium-size bowl, combine the flour, granulated sugar, baking powder, salt, cinnamon, nutmeg, and allspice; mix well and set aside.

2. In the large bowl of an electric mixer, at medium speed, beat the egg yolks with the lemon juice and 1 teaspoon oil until well combined. Beat in the milk until just blended. Gradually add the flour mixture, beating until smooth. Set aside.

3. Wash the beaters. In the clean dry small bowl of the electric mixer, at high speed, beat the egg whites until they are stiff. Fold the whites into the batter. Gently fold in the blueberries.

4. Preheat the oven to 200°F. Drop 2 or 3 large spoonfuls of batter into the hot oil and cook, turning occasionally, until the fritters are puffed and the outside is crisp and brown, about 5 minutes. (Do not undercook. The fritters will brown quickly at first but need additional cooking for the centers to cook and puff up.) Remove the fritters from the oil with a slotted spoon and drain on a paper towel–lined plate. Transfer the fritters to an ungreased baking sheet and keep warm in the oven. Repeat with the remaining batter.

5. Sift the confectioners' sugar over the fritters. Transfer the fritters to a serving plate and serve immediately.

57

A Spot of Tea with Friends

A spot of tea is always a spot of calm. Present a pot with a tray of goodies to any friend who graces your doorway, and you'll find that you have regular afternoon visitors. Or try it as the cure for a meeting that's dragging, and watch everyone loosen up around an attractive tray of brownies, lemon slices, and steaming Earl Grey. As spoons clink, smiles return. Indeed, in some countries, no social visit is complete and no business arrangement is discussed or confirmed without serving tea, a universal gesture of hospitality that expresses our urge for unity. It's hard not to be affable over tea.

For the custom of afternoon tea, we have a peckish English duchess to thank. In the early nineteenth century, Anna, the Duchess of Bedford, experienced a "sinking feeling" at about four, several hours before dinnertime. Not wishing to bestir

Above and opposite: Between sips, conversation brightens, confidences flow. Flavored blends, flowery Jasmine, or citrusy Earl Grey (which is tossed while drying with bergamot) have the gold of the afternoon in them. Or compliment your guests with Darjeeling, considered by many to be the queen of teas.

Above: Take a moment to transfer flavored honeys to pretty containers. Your friends will appreciate the extra effort.

her staff, she requested just a cup of tea with a slice of cake. Soon friends were joining her for this late afternoon delight, and the ritual spread, becoming an elaborate social gathering well sweetened with jam tarts, pastries, and even little sandwiches. (We err when we call this event "high tea," for that was the English workingman's hearty six o'clock supper.) Today, as the afternoon sun slants, you and your companions might well raise a cup to the hungry Duchess.

60

Cranberry-Orange Conserve

A conserve, a mixture of at least two fruits cooked with sugar, makes a fine spread for scones and muffins, a topping for ice cream, or a cake filling.

Makes 3 ½ cups

1 (12-ounce) package fresh or frozen cranberries

1 navel orange, coarsely chopped (including peel)

¾ cup sugar

1 cup water

½ cup toasted almonds

1. In a large nonreactive saucepan, combine the cranberries, orange, sugar, and water. Bring the mixture to a boil, stirring to dissolve the sugar. Reduce the heat and simmer, stirring occasionally, for 5 to 7 minutes, until the cranberries pop.

2. Remove the saucepan from the heat and stir in the almonds. Spoon into a serving bowl.

Stilton, Pear, and Watercress Savory Toasts

Stilton and pears are a classic combination, for a very good reason. Once you try them together, you will understand why they have been paired for nearly as long as the English have been making this famous blue cheese.

Makes 4 servings

4 slices dark rye bread, toasted

1 cup small watercress sprigs, thick stems removed

2 ripe pears, cored and sliced

8 ounces Stilton

Juice of ½ lemon

Freshly ground black pepper

Red-leaf lettuce

1. Preheat the oven to 400°F. Arrange the toast slices in a single layer in a heat-proof dish or a shallow baking pan. Layer the watercress sprigs and half the pear slices over the toast. Crumble the Stilton over the pears. Sprinkle the remaining pear slices with the lemon juice to prevent them from discoloring and set aside.

2. Bake the toast slices for 10 minutes, or until the cheese is melted and bubbling. Grind a little pepper over each. Serve the savory garnished with the red-leaf lettuce and the remaining pear slices.

Tomato and Goat Cheese Sandwiches

When you slice open an heirloom tomato, you can actually smell the sweetness from the next room. Not typically available at supermarkets, these old-fashioned varieties can be found at farmer's markets, farm stands, or in specialty catalogs. The subtle anise taste of the tarragon in these sandwiches acts as a flavor bridge to the lemony Iced Lemon Balm Tea.

Makes 4 sandwiches

¼ cup balsamic vinegar

2 to 4 small different-color ripe heirloom tomatoes

4 ounces fresh goat cheese

1 tablespoon snipped fresh chives

1 teaspoon minced fresh tarragon

½ teaspoon freshly ground black pepper

Two 4- by 4-inch slices bread, such as focaccia, cut ¼ inch thick

Salt, to taste

1 tablespoon olive oil

4 sprigs tarragon, for garnish

1. In a small saucepan, bring the balsamic vinegar to a boil and cook until reduced by two thirds. Set aside to cool.

2. Thinly slice the tomatoes. Transfer them to a paper towel–lined plate to drain.

3. In a small bowl, combine the goat cheese, chives, minced tarragon, and ¼ teaspoon pepper and blend well.

4. Spread half of the cheese mixture on one slice of the bread, top with the remaining slice of bread, and spread with the remaining cheese mixture. Arrange the slices of tomato on top of the cheese mixture, overlapping them. Sprinkle the tomatoes with salt and the remaining ¼ teaspoon pepper and drizzle with the oil and vinegar.

5. To serve, cut the sandwich into four pieces and garnish each with a sprig of tarragon.

Iced Lemon Balm Tea

Lemon balm naturally has a hint of mint and lemon, but we've intensified the flavors by adding the real things. Just as lemon and mint cleanse the palate, this tea acts as a graceful transition from scones to tarts to sandwiches on an afternoon menu. You'll never miss the caffeine, either: The tea's uplifting aroma is invigorating enough.

Makes 6 servings

1 bunch (1½ to 2 ounces) fresh lemon balm

1 small lemon, thinly sliced

4 mint tea bags

3 tablespoons honey

1. Reserve 6 sprigs of the lemon balm for garnish. Combine the remaining lemon balm, the lemon slices, and tea bags in a teapot or bowl. Pour in about 2 cups boiling water to cover. Cover and let steep for 5 minutes.

2. Remove and discard the tea bags. Stir the honey into the tea and set aside to cool to room temperature.

3. Strain the tea through a fine-meshed sieve into a large pitcher and discard the solids. Add 4 cups cold water and stir well. Refrigerate the tea until serving time.

4. Pour the chilled tea over ice in glasses. Garnish with reserved lemon balm.

Raisin and Nut Scones

Although inspired by Dundee cake, that fruity Irish delicacy made with raisins and nuts, these scones are far easier to prepare and not as filling—afternoon tea is, after all, a respite, not a meal. Clotted cream, if available, and strawberry jam are ideal toppings.

Makes about 12 scones

2 cups all-purpose flour

¼ cup sugar

4 teaspoons baking powder

5 tablespoons cold unsalted butter, cut into bits

¼ cup half-and-half

2 large eggs, lightly beaten

½ cup chopped mixed nuts

¼ cup dark raisins

1. Butter a baking sheet. Sift the flour, sugar, and baking powder into a large bowl. Add the butter and blend until the mixture resembles a coarse meal. In a small bowl, beat together the half-and-half and eggs. Stir the egg mixture into the flour mixture until just combined. Add the nuts and raisins and stir until a dough forms.

2. Turn the dough out onto a lightly floured surface and pat the dough into a ⅓-inch-thick round. With a 2½-inch floured cutter, cut out rounds. Arrange the rounds 2 inches apart on the prepared baking sheet.

3. Preheat the oven to 400°F.

4. Bake the scones for 15 to 20 minutes, until lightly golden.

Poppy Seed–Jam Tarts

Scandinavian in origin, these little tarts are a study in contrasts: delightfully crunchy poppy seeds against silky jam. If you prefer tarts without icing, just top with whipped cream right before serving.

 *Makes 16 tarts*

Poppy Seed–Jam Tarts

1 cup (2 sticks) unsalted butter, softened

½ cup granulated sugar

1 large egg yolk

1 teaspoon vanilla extract

3 tablespoons poppy seeds

2½ to 2¾ cups all-purpose flour

1 cup very thick strawberry and/or apricot jam

Icing

1 cup confectioners' sugar

About 2 tablespoons heavy cream

TO MAKE THE TARTS

1. Line a baking sheet with plastic wrap. In the large bowl of an electric mixer, at medium speed, beat the butter and granulated sugar until light and fluffy. Add the egg yolk and vanilla and continue beating until the mixture is well combined.

2. Reduce the mixer speed to low and add the poppy seeds. Gradually beat in enough of the flour to make a moderately stiff dough. Spread the dough into a 6-inch square on the prepared baking sheet and wrap it in the plastic wrap. Refrigerate the dough for a least 2 hours, or overnight.

3. Preheat the oven to 375°F. Spray sixteen 2¾- by 1-inch deep tartlet pans with nonstick cooking spray and place on a baking sheet.

4. Cut the dough into 16 equal pieces. Roll each piece into a ball. Using your fingers, press the balls into rounds, then gently press into the prepared tartlet pans, leaving an indentation in the center of the tarts for the filling. Fill each center with 1 tablespoon of the jam.

5. Bake for 12 to 15 minutes, until the edges are golden brown. Cool in the pans on wire racks. Carefully remove the tarts from the pans.

TO MAKE THE ICING

6. In a small bowl, stir together the confectioners' sugar and just enough cream to reach a piping consistency.

7. Put the icing into a pastry bag fitted with a number 1 tip. Randomly pipe a lacy pattern of icing on the tarts. Place the tarts on a serving plate and serve.

Many of us dream of working at home. Yet people who do often end up driving themselves the hardest. Their day whisks by without the quips and chats that co-workers can provide. The answer is a tea break. The custom started England's industrial revolution, when workers were bent to their tasks as early as six in the morning. Though some employers attempted to do away with this "waste of time" in the mid-nineteenth century, such was the general outcry that the workers prevailed. So steep a small pot, retrieve a cup and saucer, and renew your spirit: The tea break has a long tradition.

Left: Skip the chipped mug and enjoy your tea in a cup and saucer. You deserve it.

Citrus-Flavored Honey

Flavored honeys are easy to make and always brighten up the morning's cup of tea or muffin.

Makes 1 1/2 cups

1 (16-ounce) jar light unflavored honey
Zest of 2 lemons or oranges, cut into spirals

1. In a small saucepan, stir the honey over medium heat until it is warmed through.

2. Place the zest in a heatproof jar. Pour in the warmed honey. Cool to room temperature.

3. Cover tightly and let stand for at least 1 week before using.

The best quality tea must have creases like the leathern boot of Tartar horsemen, curl like the dewlap of a mighty bullock, unfold like a mist rising out of a ravine, gleam like a lake touched by a zephyr, and be wet and soft like a fine earth newly swept by rain.

—*The Ch'a-Ching*

Tea on the Go

Bike it, hike it, or tuck it into the beach bag: Whatever repast one totes along always tastes better outdoors than in. But just as appetites sharpen in the open air, so does thirst. And nothing both quenches and invigorates like tea.

If it's just the two of you on an autumn day, carry along a Thermos of tea and a pair of proper cups and saucers, carefully wrapped and protected in a pretty tea towel. Or, on a summer afternoon, pack a clear plastic jug and a few tea bags. With a source of clean water and a few leisurely hours, you can make sun tea (about eight tea bags to a quart), letting the heat of the sun unlock the brew's color and flavor. Prefer it chilled? Once the tea is "perked," nestle the jug between rocks in a cold mountain stream.

If you have an entire afternoon, why not pack up a full-blown picnic tea? Don't forget the Jam Cookies and refreshing Iced Clove Tea. For additional Picnic Tea menu ideas, see page 175.

Above and opposite: Even on the go, tea can be served in a proper cup. It's more civilized that way.

Currant Scones with Smoked Turkey

Small scones, split in two and filled with delectable smoked turkey and a bit of piquant apple jelly glaze, are a perfect, if slightly uncommon, combination.

Makes 12 to 14 scones

2 cups all-purpose flour

1 teaspoon cream of tartar

½ teaspoon baking soda

Pinch of salt

¼ cup vegetable shortening or margarine

⅓ cup currants

¼ cup milk

¼ cup water

Apple Tarragon Glaze

⅓ cup apple jelly

2 teaspoons chopped fresh tarragon, or ½ teaspoon dried tarragon

2 teaspoons freshly squeezed lemon juice

Filling

Butter, softened

1½ pounds thinly sliced smoked turkey

TO MAKE THE SCONES

1. Preheat the oven to 450°F. In a large bowl, sift together the flour, cream of tartar, baking soda, and salt. With a pastry blender or 2 knives, cut the shortening into the mixture until it resembles coarse meal. Toss the currants with the flour mixture.

2. In a 1-cup measuring cup, combine the milk and water. Slowly add the liquid to the flour mixture, mixing with a fork until a soft, pliable dough forms.

3. On a lightly floured surface, knead the dough gently with floured fingertips to form a smooth dough. Roll the dough out to a ½-inch thickness.

4. Cut out small hearts or other shapes, using cookie cutters about 1½ to 2 inches in diameter. Brush the tops of the scones with a little milk.

5. Heat an ungreased baking sheet in the oven until it is warm. Place the scones on the sheet and bake near the top of the oven until they are a light golden brown, about 10 minutes.

6. Remove the scones from the baking sheet and let them cool on a wire rack.

TO MAKE THE GLAZE

In a small saucepan, combine the jelly, tarragon, and lemon juice. Heat gently over medium-low heat, stirring until melted. Let the glaze cool to room temperature.

TO MAKE THE FILLING

Split the scones and butter both halves. Lay slices of turkey on the bottom half of each scone. Spread the turkey with glaze. Replace the tops of the scones and serve.

● Currant Scones with Smoked Turkey

Pumpkin Nut Bread

The whole-wheat pastry flour adds a satisfying nutty flavor to this moist pumpkin bread while maintaining a fine-crumbed texture. You can find whole-wheat pastry flour in health-food stores, or you can use triple-sifted whole-wheat flour. This will make the bread a little more densely textured.

Makes two 9-inch loaves

1 cup (2 sticks) butter, softened

2 cups packed dark-brown sugar

4 eggs

1 (16-ounce) can pumpkin puree, or 2 cups fresh pumpkin, cooked and mashed

⅓ cup molasses

2 cups all-purpose flour

2 cups whole-wheat pastry flour

1 tablespoon baking powder

½ teaspoon baking soda

1 teaspoon salt

1 teaspoon ground cinnamon

½ teaspoon freshly grated nutmeg

1½ cups toasted slivered almonds or chopped walnuts

1. Preheat the oven to 350°F. Butter two 9- by 5- by 3-inch loaf pans.

2. In the large mixing bowl of an electric mixer, cream the butter and brown sugar at medium speed until the mixture is fluffy, scraping the sides of the bowl often. Beat in the eggs, then the pumpkin and molasses. The mixture will look curdled. Set aside.

3. In another large bowl, thoroughly mix two kinds of flour, baking powder, baking soda, salt, cinnamon, and nutmeg.

4. With the mixer set at low, gradually beat the dry mixture into the pumpkin mixture, just until blended. Stir in the nuts. Pour the batter into the prepared pans.

5. Bake for 60 to 65 minutes or until a toothpick inserted in the center of a loaf comes out clean.

6. Cool the bread in the pans on wire racks for 10 minutes. Remove the loaves from the pans and let them cool completely on the racks.

Jam Cookies

Ever-popular jam-filled cookies are as fun to make as they are to eat. Stash a baggie full in your backpack or tote bag to enjoy whenever it's time for tea.

Makes 3 ½ to 4 dozen cookies

1 cup (2 sticks) butter, softened

½ cup sugar

1 egg yolk

½ teaspoon almond or vanilla extract

2½ cups all-purpose flour

⅓ cup raspberry and/or apricot jam

1. In the medium bowl of an electric mixer, beat the butter and sugar at medium speed until they are light and fluffy. Beat in the egg yolk and extract. With the mixer at low speed, gradually beat in the flour until well blended. Cover and refrigerate for at least 2 hours.

2. Preheat the oven to 350°F. Roll the chilled dough into 1-inch balls. Place them 2 inches apart on buttered baking sheets.

3. Indent the centers of each ball slightly with your thumb. Then place a rounded ¼-teaspoon measuring spoon of the jam into each depression. Pinch together any split edges on the cookies to hold in the jam.

4. Bake the cookies for 15 minutes or until they are golden. Cool on wire racks and serve.

Iced Clove Cooler

The bold flavors of cloves and cardamom and the sweet ones of ginger and allspice make a surprisingly piquant iced drink. This pairs exquisitely with savory bites such as the Currant Scones with Smoked Turkey on page 68.

Makes 6 to 8 servings

2 quarts water

16 whole cloves

5 cardamom seeds (preferably green), crushed

1 tablespoon crystallized ginger, chopped

¼ teaspoon whole allspice

6 to 8 lemon slices and mint sprigs

1. In a large saucepan, bring the water to a full boil. Add the cloves, cardamom, ginger, and allspice. Cover and let the tea stand for 7 minutes.

2. Strain the tea and let it cool to room temperature.

3. Serve the tea over ice, with lemon slices and sprigs of fresh mint.

Spicy, Soul-Warming Chai

Below: In India, chai is every-where—a folk tea, a comfort food. With this recipe at hand, enjoy it al fresco, in your own backyard.

Exotic, milky, and fragrant, chai is the ideal tea after a chilly autumn walk. The following is tea importer James Labe's quick, intensely flavorful recipe for a group: It makes twenty-four cups.

Add a quarter cup each of dried (not powdered) mace, ginger, cardamom, allspice, fennel seed, and coriander, plus two cloves, two star anise, and one cup of loose Assam tea leaves to one gallon cold water. Add three-quarters cup granulated sugar and a quarter teaspoon salt. Bring to a simmer on high heat; reduce heat to low. Add six cups whole milk and two cups half-and-half; simmer for a few minutes. Strain the chai and serve.

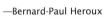

*here is no trouble so
great or grave that
cannot be much diminished
by a nice cup of tea.*

—Bernard-Paul Heroux

Relaxing with Tea at Bedtime

Supper is over, the fire lit, the book waiting. In the hours before bedtime, in Jane Austen's day, tea was an evening pleasure taken in the parlor as the family played cards or sewed and chatted. Today, when a circle of friends gathers in the evening to knit, or to discuss books or the news of the day, it is tea, sipped slowly and poured frequently, that best floats the conversation. There are many answers to what we ask of an evening's cup, but mostly that it quiet the spirit and settle the stomach, that it relax and ease us toward sleep filled with a sense of well-being.

Though India teas have the reputation of being "athletic," teas from China, which first came through England to Holland, are considered more "reflective." Among them, lettuce-pale green tea, whose fresh leaves are dried quickly (arresting the process of fermentation that gives us black teas), is not only wonderful as a palate-cleanser with food, but has gained new

Above and opposite: Tea has been considered an aid to meditation since it was first drunk in China. In Japan, its ceremonial preparation is an art form that focuses and cleanses the spirit. Let a quiet evening cup be your guide to new, profound thoughts.

73

popularity in the West because its antioxidant qualities promote health and longevity. It's a delicate sip, which needs no milk or sweeteners; or, if you prefer a touch of sweetness, try Passion Fruit Sencha.

Although tea has about 60 percent less caffeine than coffee, it does have some. Those who wish their life—or just their evenings—to be caffeine-free are among the legions who love exploring herbal and fruit teas, not least for their intriguing range of delicious flavors. Evening's most soothing teas invariably include chamomile, made from the daisy-like flower, not the leaf, of the plant. The very word (say it slowly) tastes like peace, and that is its gift. Mint, too, especially spearmint, has a relaxing and digestive effect; and for a queasy stomach, ginger tea is marvelous.

Herbal infusions, also known as tisanes, have a long medicinal history in both the East and the West. Many of Europe's

Most contemporary herbal blends mix plants deemed beneficial with tasty flavorings. The following ingredients, which promote relaxation or digestion, have various potencies, and should be enjoyed in moderation.

ALFALFA: prized for its versatile healing properties

CHAMOMILE: the queen of contentment

LAVENDER: a scented calmer

LINDEN FLOWER: woodsy and soothing, Europe's favorite

MINTS: friends of digestion

PASSION FLOWER: sweet and soothing

ST. JOHN'S WORT: counteracts the blues

Opposite: Linden and chamomile tea are so good at calming the nerves, when combined, we call them Soothing Tea.

Renaissance gardens, in fact, such as the enduringly lovely Chelsea Physic garden in London, were initially devoted to healing plants, whose salubrious powers were often ingested as teas. An infinity of tasty plants have found their way back to the teacup, to be inventively blended with everything from blackberry leaves and rose hips to lemon balm and alfalfa leaves. Dried apples, plums, or citrus peels are also zesty, popular additions, along with spices such as cinnamon or vanilla. Gone are the days when Constant Comment, that orangey old favorite, was the only choice for those who craved intense flavors in a cup!

These days, every gardener can be an herbalist. Try drying your own pesticide-free garden herbs (completely, so no moisture remains) and launch an adventure of creating your signature house blends!

Rhubarb and Ginger Jam

What a nice treat to have on hand—perfect for spreading over a simple late-night dessert of gingerbread or pound cake. You might also find yourself spreading this on toast the next morning.

Makes 8 half-pints

4 pounds trimmed rhubarb, cut into 1-inch pieces (14 cups)

6¾ cups sugar

2 teaspoons ground ginger

½ teaspoon citric acid (available at pharmacies)

1. In a heavy-bottomed 8-quart nonreactive Dutch oven, layer the rhubarb alternately with the sugar. Cover tightly and let stand in a cool place for 24 hours.

2. Stir in the ginger and citric acid. Bring the mixture to a boil over high heat, stirring to dissolve the sugar. Reduce the heat slightly but continue to boil rapidly, stirring often to prevent sticking, about 25 to 30 minutes, until the mixture is very thick—the jam should "sheet" off the spoon when it is lifted. Remove the pan from the heat; stir gently and skim off the foam.

3. Ladle the jam into 8 hot sterilized half-pint canning jars, leaving ¼ inch of headspace. Seal the jars according to the manufacturer's directions. Place the jars in a boiling water bath and process for 5 minutes after the water returns to a boil. (Add 1 minute for each 1,000 feet above sea level.)

4. Cool the jars on a wire rack. Store them in a cool dry dark place.

Soothing Tea

Linden leaves and flowers (sometimes called basswood or lime) are legendary for calming the nerves and promoting restful sleep.

Makes 4 to 6 servings

1 tablespoon pesticide-free linden leaves and flowers

1 tablespoon pesticide-free chamomile

1 tablespoon fragrant pesticide-free rose petals

1. Pour boiling water into the teapot and set aside for 5 minutes. Discard the water.

2. Gently crush the linden leaves and flowers, chamomile and rose petals to release their flavor. Put them into a tea ball, cover the tea ball, and place in the teapot. Cover with boiling water and let steep for 5 minutes.

3. Remove the tea ball from the teapot. Serve the tea immediately.

Orange-Marmalade Cake

Real orange syrup locked into the butter-milk-rich layers tenderize this homespun cake. The Soothing Tea perfectly complements this light, citrusy dessert. Any mild green tea would also suit, or even a first-flush Darjeeling such as Mim, a delicate spring harvest tea with a hint of white grapes and a flowery aroma.

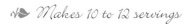 *Makes 10 to 12 servings*

Orange Cake

3 cups cake flour

½ teaspoon baking soda

½ teaspoon salt

1 cup (2 sticks) softened unsalted butter

2 cups sugar

3 large eggs, at room temperature, lightly beaten

1 tablespoon grated orange zest

1½ teaspoons vanilla extract

1 cup buttermilk, at room temperature

Orange Syrup

1 cup fresh orange juice

¼ cup sugar

Marmalade Filling

1 cup orange marmalade

Sour Cream Frosting

¾ cup well-chilled heavy cream

3 tablespoons sugar

¾ cup well-chilled sour cream

TO MAKE THE ORANGE CAKE

1. Preheat the oven to 325°F. Butter two 9-inch round cake pans, line them with parchment paper, and butter and flour the paper, shaking out the excess.

2. Sift together the flour, baking soda, and salt into a large bowl.

3. In the large bowl of an electric mixer, at medium-high speed, beat the butter until creamy. Add the sugar a little at a time and beat the mixture until light and fluffy. Beat in the eggs, orange zest, and vanilla. Add the flour, alternately with the buttermilk in three additions, beating after each addition just until smooth.

4. Divide the batter between the prepared pans, smoothing the surface, and rap each pan on the counter to burst any air pockets. Bake for 45 minutes, or until a toothpick inserted in the center comes out clean. Transfer the cakes to wire racks to cool for 20 minutes.

TO MAKE THE ORANGE SYRUP

5. Meanwhile, in a medium-size bowl, stir together the orange juice and sugar until the sugar is dissolved.

6. With a toothpick, poke holes at ½-inch intervals in the cake layers. Gradually spoon the syrup over the layers, allowing each addition to be completely absorbed before adding more syrup. Let the layers cool completely.

TO MAKE THE MARMALADE FILLING

7. In a small saucepan over medium heat, heat the marmalade until just melted. Set aside to cool for 5 minutes.

TO MAKE THE SOUR CREAM FROSTING

8. In a medium-size bowl, whisk the heavy cream with the sugar until it forms firm peaks. Add the sour cream a little at a time and whisk until the frosting resembles a spreadable consistency.

9. Invert one of the layers onto a cake plate and carefully peel off the parchment paper. Spread two thirds of the marmalade filling over the top, smoothing it evenly. Invert the remaining cake layer onto the top of the first one and peel off the parchment paper. Spoon the remaining marmalade onto the top, leaving a 1¼-inch border with the sour cream frosting, leaving the marmalade exposed. Chill for at least 2 hours before serving.

Tea and a Good Book

There is no better company than tea when you settle down to read of other times, other lives, and find yourself there.

Pilgrim at Tinker Creek ▪ Annie Dillard
Essays that plumb nature and the spirit.

Eat, Pray, Love ▪ Elizabeth Gilbert
One woman's search for meaning across Italy, India, and Indonesia.

The Lace Reader ▪ Brunonia Barry
A descendant of mind readers confronts foul play.

To the Lighthouse ▪ Virginia Woolf
Mrs. Ramsay's household, Woolf's masterpiece.

Tell Me a Story ▪ Tillie Olsen
Three stories that unfold the depths in women's daily lives.

Pride and Prejudice ▪ Jane Austen
Who is immune to Mr. Darcy's charms?

Rebecca ▪ Daphne du Maurier
A second wife haunted by the mystery of the first.

Lark Rise to Candleford ▪ Flora Thompson
The postmistress's view of English village life.

Tender Is the Night ▪ F. Scott Fitzgerald
Cavorting on the French Riviera in the 1920s.

Possession ▪ A.A. Byatt
A Victorian poet's romance, uncovered by a scholar.

Talk Before Sleep ▪ Elizabeth Berg
A tender, sad-funny story of women who gather to help a dying friend.

The Guernsey Literary and Potato Peel Pie Society ▪ Mary Ann Schaffer and Annie Barrows
A celebration of the power of books to nourish people through difficult times.

The Selected Poems of Emily Dickinson
Poems forever fresh that search the soul.

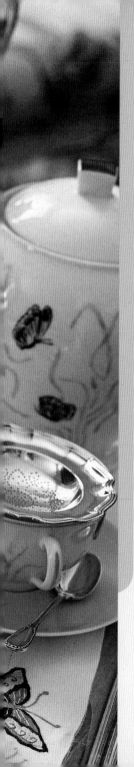

Tea and Special Occasions

Bring out the best cups and dessert plates—company is coming for tea! The appeal of a tea party has particular resonance in our hurried modern lives: A sweet indulgence held at a civilized hour, a way to fête all ages, a relaxing respite from the everyday—a tea party honors our guests with a graceful touch of ceremony.

Opposite: If the china you inherited or received as a wedding gift is collecting dust, a formal tea party is the perfect opportunity to use it. In fact, why not host a smashing tea party for the same special occasion each year? It will become your signature event.

> *"Take some more tea," the March Hare said to Alice very earnestly. "I've had nothing yet," Alice replied in an offended tone: "so I can't take more." "You mean you can't take less," said the Hatter: "it's very easy to take more than nothing."*
>
> —Lewis Carroll, *Alice in Wonderland*

A Children's Tea Party

They may bounce on their beds and hang by their knees, but all kids enjoy pretending to be grown-ups. It's a wish worth indulging with a children's tea party, for along with yummy things to eat comes a lesson in good-hostess graces, from pouring the lemonade to making sure all the guests are having a good time.

One birthday idea is a dress-up tea party, at which both boys and girls can rummage through old-fashioned garb (including loopy beads and outrageous bow-ties) gleaned from thrift shops to assemble their own costumes. Hat decorating is a great party game. All it requires are some plain hats and lots of ribbon, scarves, or snippets, silk flowers, and glue; each child dons his or her fabulous creation for teatime and then gets to wear it home.

Above and opposite: For a summertime tea in the garden, young hostesses invent with what's on hand: mint in abundance for the iced tea, a watering pot for a fresh-plucked bouquet. No need to be formal here, where butterflies arrive uninvited.

A child-sized tea set would make teatime more manageable for revelers with small hands.

Honey Tea Sandwiches

Straight from the heart of the Cotswolds, this recipe involves baking your own honey quick bread and cutting it into decorative shapes. The simple sandwich filling is a silky mix of lemon and banana.

Makes 6 or 7 sandwiches

¾ cup hot strong brewed tea

¾ cup packed brown sugar

⅓ cup honey

2 cups unbleached all-purpose flour

1½ teaspoons baking soda

1 banana

1 teaspoon fresh lemon juice

Chocolate drop candies or colored sprinkles, for garnish

1. Preheat the oven to 350°F. Butter and flour an 8½- by 4½- by 2½-inch loaf pan.

2. Divide the tea between two small bowls. Stir the brown sugar into one bowl until dissolved. Stir the honey into the other bowl until dissolved. Set both bowls aside.

3. In a medium-size bowl, combine the flour and baking soda. Stir in the sugar-tea mixture until blended. Quickly stir in the honey-tea mixture until blended. Pour the batter into the prepared pan.

4. Bake for 40 to 45 minutes, until a toothpick inserted in the center comes out clean. Cool the bread in the pan on a wire rack for 10 minutes. Remove from the pan and cool the bread on a wire rack.

5. In a medium-size bowl, mash the banana with the lemon juice.

6. Trim off the ends of the bread. Cut the loaf into ½-inch-thick slices. With a 1¾- to 2-inch cookie cutter, cut a flower shape from each slice. With a sharp paring knife or a very small round cookie cutter, cut a ½-inch hole in the center of half the flowers.

7. Spread the solid bread flowers with the banana mixture. Top with the remaining slices. Fill the holes with the chocolate drops. Serve at once.

Vanilla Milk Tea

Here is just the sort of velvety-sweet tea served in an English nursery at midday to help sustain children through energetic afternoons. This recipe calls for English breakfast, a blend of black teas from Ceylon and India, which is tailor-made to go with milk (as are all black teas).

Makes 4 to 5 servings

1 cup milk

One 2-inch piece vanilla bean, split

4 teaspoons English breakfast tea

1. Pour the milk into a small saucepan. Add the split vanilla bean and bring to a simmer, stirring often. Remove the saucepan from the heat and let stand until the milk is cool. Remove the vanilla bean.

2. Brew the tea according to the package directions. Pour the tea into warmed mugs and top with the vanilla milk.

Lemon Cupcakes

Dressed up with sprigs of herbs, these elegant cupcakes can be served to children and adults with equal success.

Makes 21 cupcakes

½ cup milk

¼ cup chopped fresh lemon balm, lemon thyme, or lemon verbena

2 teaspoons grated lemon zest

3 tablespoons fresh lemon juice

2 cups sifted all-purpose flour

½ teaspoon baking soda

¼ teaspoon salt

½ cup (1 stick) softened unsalted butter

1¼ cups granulated sugar

2 large egg yolks, at room temperature

3 large egg whites, at room temperature, stiffly beaten

2 cups confectioners' sugar

2 tablespoons heavy cream

Lemon balm, lemon thyme, or lemon verbena sprigs, for garnish (optional)

1. Preheat the oven to 350°F. Butter and flour twenty-one 2½-inch muffin cups or line them with paper muffin cups.

2. In a small saucepan, combine the milk and lemon balm. Bring to just under a simmer over medium heat. Remove the saucepan from the heat and let steep until the milk has cooled. Strain the milk through a fine-meshed sieve into a small bowl; discard the solids. Stir the lemon zest and 1 tablespoon lemon juice into the milk (the mixture will curdle); set aside.

3. In a medium-size bowl, stir together the flour, baking soda, and salt.

4. In the small bowl of an electric mixer, at medium speed, cream the butter. Gradually add the granulated sugar, beating until the mixture is light and fluffy. Add the egg yolks one at a time, beating well after each addition. Add the flour mixture alternately with the milk mixture, beating until smooth after each addition. Gently fold in the egg whites. Spoon the batter into the muffin cups, filling them halfway.

5. Bake for 15 to 18 minutes, until a toothpick inserted in the center comes out clean. Remove the cupcakes from the pans and cool completely on wire racks.

6. Sift the confectioners' sugar into the medium-size bowl of an electric mixer. With the mixer at medium speed, gradually add the cream and the remaining 2 tablespoons lemon juice. Beat the icing until it is smooth and spreadable.

7. Frost the cooled cupcakes with the icing. Transfer to a platter and garnish the cupcakes with fresh herbs, if desired.

Lemon Cupcakes

Tea and Good Company

Tea is like a hug and a handshake; something about it warms friendships and inspires confidences. Though we don't always stand on ceremony with good friends—mugs will do for that marathon chat at the kitchen table—it's also fun to honor them with the flourish of a tea nicely presented. Whether you invite four or fourteen to tea, stick to what works best for your own home and personal style. Though in an earlier day the hostess poured, asking each guest in turn his or her preference, you might let them fix their own tea (made ahead very strong) and dilute it with hot water to taste. Small tables within reach—no one really likes balancing a cup or saucer on a knee—and miniature, varied delectables that fingers or little plates can handle gracefully help put everyone at ease.

Above and opposite: Remember your childhood view of a tea party—pinkies raised, everyone stiff and formal? Yet a grown-up tea can be the most relaxed of gatherings, a time for laughter and sharing. The point of a party among good friends is the company itself, and the pleasure of feeling everyone's spirits rising with the tea steam.

Celebrate the strawberry season and a warm day with a picnic tea party. Pack a Thermos of tea, iced or hot, fresh berries and scones, dishes muffled in cloth napkins, and venture out of doors. You don't have to hike up a mountain to appreciate the manna that tea—thirst-quenching, restorative, and sweetened as you like—is to wanderers.

English Scones

The remarkable thing about scones is that on their own they are the simplest of plain risen cakes. But lavish on the jam and clotted cream (or lashings of butter) and they become quite sumptuous indeed. For best results, bake these just before your party.

Makes about 8 scones

1⅔ cups self-rising cake flour

½ teaspoon baking powder

2 tablespoons sugar

½ teaspoon salt

¼ cup (½ stick) cold unsalted butter, cut into bits

1 large egg

½ cup plus 2 tablespoons milk, plus additional for glazing

Fresh jam and clotted cream, for serving

1. Preheat the oven to 425°F. Butter a baking sheet.
2. Sift the flour, baking powder, sugar, and salt together into a medium-size bowl. With a pastry blender or two knives, cut in the butter until the mixture resembles a coarse meal.
3. In a small bowl, beat together the egg and milk. Add the milk mixture a little at a time to the dry ingredients, stirring until a sticky dough forms.
4. Turn the dough out onto a lightly floured surface and roll it into a ¾-inch-thick round. Cut out the scones with a floured 2-inch cookie cutter. Arrange the scones about 1 inch apart on the prepared baking sheet and brush the tops with milk.
5. Bake the scones for 12 to 15 minutes, until the tops are lightly golden and the bottoms sound hollow when tapped.
6. Serve the scones on a platter with the jam and clotted cream on the side.

Blackberry Iced Tea

The rich, deep flavors of orange pekoe and Darjeeling teas both lend themselves to the tartness of blackberries, but don't restrict yourself to this union. Try different kinds of fruit-and-tea combinations; for instance, sliced fresh peaches with amber-colored Formosa oolong, which boasts a taste that has been likened to ripe peaches.

Makes about 4 servings

½ to 1 ounce pesticide-free marigold flowers

4 cups hot black tea, such as orange pekoe or Darjeeling

1 cup blackberries

Honey, to taste

1. Remove the petals from the flowers.
2. Place 3 to 4 petals in each compartment of an ice-cube tray. Fill the compartments halfway with water and freeze for at least 2 hours. Fill each compartment to the top with water and freeze until solid.

3. In a medium-size bowl, combine the hot tea with the blackberries. Set aside to steep for 1 hour.

4. With the back of a wooden spoon, crush the berries against the side of the bowl. Pour the mixture through a fine-meshed sieve into a pitcher, pressing on the solids with the back of the spoon to extract all the liquid; discard the solids. Add honey to taste and chill for at least 2 hours.

5. Serve in tall glasses with the marigold ice cubes.

Amuse-bouches, or bite-size canapés, both tempt the appetite and enhance a buffet display. Choose a mild goat cheese, such as Montrachet or Chavrous.

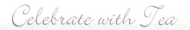 *Makes 16 to 20 toasts*

½ loaf French bread (baguette), cut into ¼-inch-thick slices

1 (11-ounce) log goat cheese, cut into ¼-inch-thick slices

2 tablespoons extra-virgin olive oil

Pink peppercorns

Leaves from ½ bunch fresh thyme

1. Preheat the broiler. Arrange the bread slices on an ungreased baking sheet. Broil the bread 3 to 4 inches from the heat for 1 to 2 minutes, until toasted.

2. Turn the slices over, top with the goat cheese, drizzle lightly with the oil, and sprinkle each toast with a few peppercorns and thyme leaves. Broil for 1½ to 2 minutes, until the cheese is warm and the edges of the bread are toasted.

Celebrate with Tea

Here are some more perfect excuses to throw a tea party.

Your mother or sister has come to visit: Invite your friends to meet her.

A play (or concert or benefit drive) is a huge success: Have the whole gang over for thanks, reunion—and tea.

Long-time friends are leaving the neighborhood: Let them know how much they'll be missed at a tea to which everyone contributes a confection.

Your best friend is expecting a child: Host a shower in her honor.

You want to start a book group: Invite everyone interested to meet each other and work out the game plan.

The garden has never been lovelier: Put chairs and tables outside and share the splendid results of your labors.

Hold a gourmet tea-tasting: Let each guest bring her favorite tea (and her own pot) and invite her to tell the others all about her choice.

Cucumber-Basil Tea Sandwiches

Cucumber-Basil Tea Sandwiches

Basil complements the sweetness of English cucumber, making these traditional tea sandwiches something special. To make them even fancier, "frill" the cucumber by drawing a fork lengthwise down the vegetable before slicing.

Makes 24 sandwiches

1 (8-ounce) package softened cream cheese

2 tablespoons half-and-half

2 tablespoons snipped fresh chives

1 unsliced loaf or 12 slices rye or whole-wheat bread

1 English (seedless) cucumber, cut into thin slices

24 fresh basil leaves

1. In a medium-size bowl, beat together the cream cheese and half-and-half until it is the consistency of soft butter. Stir in the chives.

2. If you are using an unsliced loaf of bread, slice 12 thin slices from it. Spread the cheese mixture on half the bread slices, then top each with several slices of cucumber, a basil leaf, and the rest of the bread. Cut into quarters and serve the sandwiches immediately, or cover with plastic wrap and refrigerate until ready to serve.

Butter Sponge Cake

A variation on the rich Victorian sponge cake, this lighter version omits the buttercream and cuts the cake in half: Rather than two separate baked layers, it is made of one layer sliced into two extra-delicate tiers. Try serving Badamtam, a grand Darjeeling and wonderful tea party beverage, with this.

Makes 6 to 8 servings

¾ cup (1½ sticks) softened unsalted butter

¾ cup granulated sugar

3 large eggs

1½ cups all-purpose flour

1 teaspoon vanilla extract

1½ teaspoons baking powder

Raspberry jam, to taste

Confectioners' sugar, for dusting

1. Preheat the oven to 350°F. Butter and flour an 8-inch round cake pan.

2. In the medium bowl of an electric mixer, at medium speed, cream the butter and granulated sugar until light and fluffy. Add the eggs one at a time, adding 1 tablespoon of flour with each egg, and beating after each addition until well combined. Stir in the vanilla.

3. Sift the remaining flour and the baking powder into a medium-size bowl. Stir the dry ingredients into the butter mixture until blended. Pour the batter into the prepared pan, spreading it evenly.

4. Bake for 45 to 50 minutes, until a toothpick inserted in the center comes out clean.

5. Let the cake cool in the pan on a wire rack for 5 minutes. Invert the cake onto the wire rack and let it cool completely.

6. Using a serrated knife, cut the cake horizontally into two layers. Spread the raspberry jam over the bottom layer, then top with the remaining layer. Place a doily over the cake and sift a dusting of confectioners' sugar over the top. Remove the doily and serve.

Bay Leaf Honey

The pungent, woodsy aroma and faint cinnamon taste of bay leaf make it a nice, slightly spicy addition to honey. Drizzle this in your tea or spread it over scones or biscuits.

Makes 2 cups

2 cups light unflavored honey

1 large bay leaf

1. In a small saucepan over low heat, stir the honey until warmed through. Place the bay leaf in a sterilized jar and pour in the warmed honey.

2. Cover and let stand for at least 1 week before using.

Ruby Tea Biscuits

Though these gleaming biscuits (ruby red from the jam or jelly) could crown the fanciest tables, they're also wonderful to serve at a last-minute informal lunch. They can be made in a pinch because most of the ingredients are already in your kitchen, and you can top them with any kind of red preserve you like (cranberry, raspberry, and red currant are all delicious possibilities).

Makes 12 biscuits

2 cups sifted all-purpose flour

2 tablespoons sugar

4 teaspoons baking powder

½ teaspoon salt

½ cup vegetable shortening

¾ cup milk

2 tablespoons red jam or jelly

1. Place an oven rack in the center of the oven. Preheat the oven to 425°F.

2. In a large mixing bowl, combine the flour, sugar, baking powder, and salt. Mix well with a fork. With a pastry blender or two knives, cut in the shortening until the mixture resembles a coarse meal. Add the milk and mix with a fork just until the dough forms a soft ball.

3. Turn the dough out onto a floured surface and lightly knead 12 times with floured hands. Flour a rolling pin and roll out the dough ¼ inch thick. With a floured 2-inch round cookie cutter, cut out the biscuits.

4. Using a spatula, lift half the circles, one at a time, onto an ungreased baking sheet, arranging them about 1 inch apart.

5. With a floured 1-inch round cutter, cut a hole in the center of the remaining biscuits to make rings. Lift out the dough centers with the spatula and set aside. With the spatula, place the rings on top of the dough circles on the cookie sheet.

6. Carefully fill the middle of each ring with ½ teaspoon jam.

7. Bake for 12 to 15 minutes, until the biscuits are puffed and lightly golden. Transfer the biscuits to wire racks to cool slightly. If desired, bake the 1-inch centers for 10 to 12 minutes, until lightly golden.

8. Serve the biscuits on warm plates.

 Ruby Tea Biscuits

A Novel Tea Party

It is a truth universally acknowledged that conversation flows happily over tea. Ah, yes...but which tea, exactly? If your book club has planned to discuss an English novel of manners—the sort of gentle domestic drama that flows from Jane Austen to Barbara Pym—why not cue the tea to the genre, perhaps offering a delicate Darjeeling in porcelain cups with petite sandwiches of smoked salmon and curried egg salad? Or go all out and serve a classic English tea—an authentic menu appears on page 138.

Whodunit?
Death on the Nile ▪ Agatha Christie
The Daughter of Time ▪ Josephine Tey
Serve English breakfast tea and fruit scones.

Biography
Secrets of the Flesh: A Life of Collette ▪ Judith Thurman
Everybody Was So Young ▪ Amanda Vaill
Serve oolong and madeleines.

Classics
Madame Bovary ▪ Gustave Flaubert
To the Lighthouse ▪ Virginia Woolf
Serve Darjeeling and lemon cake.

Distant Lands
The Poisonwood Bible ▪ Barbara Kingsolver
Corelli's Mandolin ▪ Louis de Bernières
Serve orange pekoe and pita with eggplant puree.

Women's Lives
Tell Me a Riddle ▪ Tillie Olsen
Final Payments ▪ Mary Gordon
Serve chamomile and fruit tartlets.

It's natural to pair books with sips and snacks. After all, so much literature is drenched in tea, from Henry James to Rosamunde Pilcher. Your book-mates will love the connection.

97

In the South, you can't marry a man until you know how his Mama makes sweet tea.

—Sandra Chastain et al., *Sweet Tea and Jesus Shoes*

"Here Comes the Bride" Shower

Now that the news is out, her smile shines even brighter than the stone in her engagement ring. It's a time when she longs to share her joy with all her friends. A tea for a bride-to-be is one of the happiest of all events—a reunion about union—and deserves your best efforts. Collaborate with the engaged couple's parents to pilfer childhood pictures of both (scan hers onto the invitations, display his around the room), and plot some heartfelt mischief for a wedding shower tea party, such as silly souvenirs (her camp archery award, framed as a Cupid's gift for him; his kindergarten report card for her). Invite her oldest friend to dredge up memories of their shared child-hood; or, if you dare, ask the groom twenty questions ahead of time—and see if she can guess his answers! Though you may not want to make the party itself a surprise, some guests can be—especially a dear friend from far away.

Opposite and above: Neither a luncheon nor a dinner, an afternoon tea invites imagination to the table. When love is the theme, use flowers and herbs that once relayed symbolic messages: rosemary for remembrance, roses for passions, violets for fidelity.

99

Opposite: When it comes to engagement parties, it's impossible to be too romantic. Set the table, or a variety of small tables, with your finest china, or use those beautifully mismatched little plates, teacups, and saucers you've collected over the years, and indulge everyone with confections as artful as they are delicious.

Below: Guests will be charmed by a miniature version of your wedding cake and heart-shaped sugar cookies.

For this occasion, choose a soft, romantic color theme for table linens, candles, placecards, and flowers, and don't be shy about asking to borrow a friend's pretty cake stand or silver teapot. A well-organized hostess gets others to contribute—and they'll want to. When guests arrive, it's thoughtful to have tea and plates of cookies or pastries ready to greet them, even if you intend to serve little sandwiches later—it warms up the party while you wait for the late-comers, and gives the bride-to-be a chance to visit with everyone.

When it comes to gifts, why not make them themed to tea? Silver teaspoons, pretty cups, a needlepoint tea caddy, or some crochet-edged napkins—they'll remind the bride of this gathering always, and inspire her to invite you all for tea after the wedding.

Tea and Sweet Gratitude

A bride is the recipient of so much kindness that sometimes mere thank-you notes hardly seem adequate. For a heart overflowing with gratitude, an after-the-wedding tea is a meaningful way of showing appreciation to well-wishers of all generations. (Your parents' friends will be especially touched to be invited.)

Serve a small copy of the wedding cake and romantic cookies that indicate "love is flourishing," and by all means use your guests' gifts, including every piece of that wedding-present china! A golden tea "Bellini" punch would be a sophisticated touch, too: Just fill a punch bowl with white wine and soda water (as if making a wine spritzer), add peach juice, tea, and some fresh strawberries.

100

Watercress and Nasturtium Sandwiches

If you have a few extra minutes before company arrives, make these sandwiches even fancier: Dip the edges of the watercress sprigs used for garnish into paprika.

Makes 16 sandwiches

1 large bunch watercress

30 pesticide-free nasturtium flowers

1 (8-ounce) package softened cream cheese

½ cup peeled, seeded, and finely chopped cucumber

2 to 4 tablespoons very finely chopped yellow onion, to taste

¼ teaspoon salt

⅛ teaspoon freshly ground black pepper

8 slices fine-grained country white, wheat, or egg bread

1. Reserve 16 watercress sprigs for garnish. Chop enough of the remaining watercress leaves to make ½ cup. Reserve 8 nasturtium flowers for garnish. Cut the remaining nasturtium flowers into a fine julienne. Set both aside.

2. In a medium-size bowl, combine the cream cheese, cucumber, onion, chopped watercress, julienned nasturtium flowers, salt, and pepper. Mix well. Cover the mixture with plastic wrap and let stand for 1 hour to allow the flavors to blend.

3. Generously spread the cream cheese mixture onto the bread slices. Cut the sandwiches in half and transfer them to a serving plate. Just before serving, garnish with the reserved watercress sprigs and nasturtium flowers.

Smoked Salmon Canapés

Just as semisweet, delicate wines are traditionally served with smoked fish, these salmon appetizers are a wonderful foil for Strawberry Iced Tea, subtly lightened with lemon, sugar, and strawberries. If you can't get tobiko, substitute golden (whitefish) caviar.

Makes 12 canapés

6 slices dark rye cocktail bread

2 ounces thinly sliced smoked salmon

2 (3-ounce) packages cream cheese with chives, softened

About 2 tablespoons tobiko (flying fish roe, available at Japanese markets), for garnish

Dill sprigs, for garnish

1. Cut each slide of bread diagonally in half. Decoratively top each piece of bread with a thick strip of salmon.

2. Place the cream cheese in a pastry bag fitted with a number 1M tip. Pipe a rosette of cream cheese on top of each piece of salmon.

3. Transfer the canapés to serving plates. Just before serving, garnish each canapé with a small spoonful of tobiko and a sprig of dill.

Rose Petal Scones

Inspired by Middle Eastern cooking, these pretty, delicate scones are flavored with rose water and pistachios.

Makes about 24 scones

2¼ cups all-purpose flour

2 teaspoons granulated sugar

2 teaspoons baking powder

½ teaspoon baking soda

¾ teaspoon salt

⅛ teaspoon ground cinnamon

¼ cup (½ stick) cold unsalted butter, cut into bits

⅓ cup shelled and peeled pistachios, lightly toasted and coarsely ground

1 cup heavy cream

1 teaspoon rose water

2 tablespoons thinly sliced pesticide-free rose petals

1 cup confectioners' sugar

1 tablespoon rose jelly, or 1 tablespoon red currant jelly mixed with ½ teaspoon rose water

2 to 3 teaspoons water

1. Preheat the oven to 425°F. Lightly butter a baking sheet.

2. Sift the flour, sugar, baking power, baking soda, salt, and cinnamon together into a large bowl. With a pastry blender or two knives, cut in the butter until the mixture resembles a coarse meal. Stir in the pistachios.

3. In a small bowl, combine the cream, rose water, and rose petals. Add to the flour mixture and stir to form a soft dough.

4. Place the dough in heaping tablespoon-fuls about 1 inch apart on the prepared baking sheet. Bake for 10 to 12 minutes, until scones are golden brown. Transfer the scones to a wire rack set over a jelly-roll pan.

5. In a medium-size bowl, whisk together the confectioners' sugar, jelly, and water until smooth, adding more water if needed. Drizzle the icing over the warm scones. Serve immediately.

Rose Petal Scones (shown at top).

Heart Cookies

For a dotted-swiss look that mimics bridal finery, pipe the icing out of small pastry bags, making tiny circlets.

Makes 48 cookies

2½ cups all-purpose flour

½ teaspoon salt

1 cup (2 sticks) unsalted butter, softened

⅔ cup granulated sugar

1 large egg

2 cups confectioners' sugar

About ¼ cup milk

Food coloring (optional)

1. In a medium-size bowl, stir together the flour and salt. Set aside.

2. In the large bowl of an electric mixer, at medium speed, cream the butter and granulated sugar until light and fluffy. Add the egg and mix until blended. Gradually beat in the flour mixture at low speed, just until blended.

3. Divide the dough in half. Form each half into a disk and wrap in plastic wrap. Refrigerate the dough for 2 hours.

4. Preheat the oven to 350°F.

5. On a lightly floured surface, roll out the dough ⅛ inch thick. With a 2½-inch heart-shaped cookie cutter, cut out as many hearts as possible. Arrange hearts 1 inch apart on ungreased baking sheets.

6. Bake for 7 to 8 minutes, until the cookies start to brown.

7. Meanwhile, sift the confectioners' sugar into a medium-size bowl. Stir enough of the milk to form an icing with a runny consistency. Add the food coloring to tint the icing, if desired.

8. Spread the icing on the hot cookies. Cool the iced cookies on wire racks placed over waxed paper.

Strawberry Iced Tea

If you don't want to use tea bags, sprinkle the juice from 2 or 3 strawberries pressed through a fine-meshed sieve onto 3 to 4 teaspoons loose tea leaves, allow them to dry, and then brew them. The touch of lemon cuts through the strawberry-and-sugar sweetness.

Makes 2 to 3 servings

2 cups water

2 strawberry tea bags

¼ cup sugar

Juice of half a lemon

Strawberries, for garnish

1. In a large saucepan, bring the water to a full boil. Add the tea bags and sugar. Remove the saucepan from the heat, cover, and let steep for 5 minutes.

2. Remove and discard the tea bags. Stir the lemon juice into the tea mixture and cool to room temperature.

3. Serve over crushed ice, garnished with strawberries.

Iced Darjeeling and Fruit Tea

Only teas grown on the gentle slopes of Darjeeling, India, bear this special title. Darjeeling complements a wide range of foods, while also being flavorful enough to drink alone.

Makes 6 to 8 servings

2 quarts water

8 teaspoons Darjeeling tea

1 cup sugar

5 whole cloves

Zest and juice of 1 orange

Zest and juice of 1 lime

Lime wedges, for garnish

1. In a medium-size saucepan, bring 1 quart water to a full boil. Add the tea, remove the saucepan from the heat, cover, and let stand for 5 minutes. Strain the mixture through a fine-meshed sieve into a large bowl; discard the solids. Cover and refrigerate the tea for at least 2 hours, or overnight.

2. In another medium-size saucepan, bring the remaining 1 quart water to a full boil. Add the sugar, cloves, and orange and lime zests. Bring the mixture back to a boil and cook for 5 minutes. Remove the saucepan from the heat and stir in the orange and lime juices.

3. Strain the sugar mixture through a fine-meshed sieve into the tea mixture. Cool to room temperature.

4. Serve the tea over crushed ice, garnished with the lime wedges.

Rose Petal Jam

Not entirely a jam but more like a pourable "honey" in consistency, this ambrosial topping for toast, muffins, or vanilla ice cream is best made with rose water, an intensely fragrant essence that must be used sparingly.

Makes 1 1/4 cups

1 1/2 cups lightly packed pesticide-free rose petals

1 1/2 cups water

1 1/3 cups sugar

1/4 cup fresh lemon juice

1 teaspoon rose water (optional)

1. Spread the rose petals out on a paper towel–lined plate. Snip out the bitter white heels and any brown spots on the petals.

2. In a large heavy-bottomed saucepan, combine the rose petals and water. Stir in the sugar, lemon juice, and rose water, if desired. Bring to a full rolling boil over medium-high heat, stirring constantly.

3. Reduce the heat to medium and continue to cook, stirring often to prevent sticking, for 25 to 30 minutes, until the mixture thickens. When the mixture is done, a spoonful of jam will hold its shape when placed on a cold plate.

4. Remove the jam from the heat and ladle into two sterilized 6-ounce jars. Cover the tops with melted paraffin and store in a cool, dark place for up to 2 weeks.

A Heart-Warming Holiday Tea

There's no better time to have a party than when the house is spiced with pine boughs, the silver gleams, and a ribboned wreath adorns the door. Whether it's a tree-trimming party by the fire or an afternoon open house, a holiday tea is the perfect way to include entire families, from toddlers to grandparents. It's good to have a punch table for the little ones, with snatchable sweets like sugar cookies that won't bring disaster to a velvet dress. As a surprise, you might sit them down for a special holiday cake, or follow old family customs such as baking coins into a steamed pudding. A hot tea spiced with cinnamon and orange adds a festive aroma to the gathering. And with sherry and port on the sideboard, as well as sweets and savories to last the lingering hours, you'll have truly shared a merry time with all.

Opposite and above: When it's late on Christmas Eve, and yet more ribbons need tying, a tea break is in order. As carols play, sit back for a moment and sip—it may help you remember where you hid the presents you can't seem to find.

Invite friends and family to sip tea, munch on cookies, and enjoy the warmth and comfort of your home and each other's company.

Sorrel, Leek, and Mushroom Tart

Slightly sour sorrel leaves are tempered by rich eggs, cheese, and cream in this savory French tart—a traditional dish for celebrations.

Makes 6 to 8 servings

Tart Shell

1½ cups all-purpose flour

¾ teaspoons salt

6 tablespoons (¾ stick) cold unsalted butter, cut into bits

2 tablespoons solid white shortening

3 to 4 tablespoons ice water

Sorrel, Leek, and Mushroom Filling

3 tablespoons unsalted butter

1 large leek, white part only, finely chopped (1 cup)

¼ pound cremini or white button mushrooms, thinly sliced

1 teaspoon fresh thyme

½ teaspoon salt

4 ounces sorrel or spinach, stemmed and sliced into thin ribbons

3 large eggs

1 cup heavy cream

½ cup grated Gruyère or Comtè cheese

⅛ teaspoon freshly ground black pepper

TO MAKE THE TART SHELL

1. In a medium-size bowl, combine the flour and salt. With a pastry blender or two knives, cut in the butter and shortening until the mixture resembles a coarse meal.

2. Gradually add the ice water, tossing with a fork until the dough just clings together. Flatten the dough into a disk and wrap in plastic wrap. Refrigerate for at least 30 minutes.

3. Preheat the oven to 425°F.

4. On a lightly floured surface, roll out the dough to a 13-inch circle. Fit it into a 9-inch tart pan. Trim to ½ inch above the edge of the pan and flute the edge. Place the tart pan on a baking sheet. Line the tart shell with a double thickness of aluminum foil and fill with dried beans.

5. Bake the shell for 10 minutes. Remove the aluminum foil and beans. Using a fork, prick any puffy areas, and bake for 4 to 5 minutes longer, until the edges start to brown. Cool on a wire rack. Reduce the oven temperature to 375°F.

TO MAKE THE SORREL, LEEK, AND MUSHROOM FILLING

6. In a large skillet over medium heat, melt the butter. Add the leek and sauté until tender. Add the mushrooms, thyme, and salt. Sauté until the liquid from the mushrooms has evaporated.

7. Add the sorrel, stirring quickly, just until wilted, about 1 minute. Remove from the heat and let cool.

8. In a medium-size bowl, whisk the eggs and cream until well combined. Stir in the cheese, pepper, and leek mixture.

9. Pour the filling into the cooled pastry shell, spreading it evenly. Place the tart on a baking sheet and bake for 35 to 40 minutes, until the filling is firm and golden brown.

10. Cool the tart on a wire rack for 20 to 30 minutes before serving.

Garlic-Herb Cheese

This flavorful spread is even more enticing when pressed through a pastry tube to create appealing designs on top of open-faced tea sandwiches or crackers. This cheese improves in flavor after a day and may be kept for 2 to 3 days, covered and chilled. Bring to room temperature before serving.

Makes about 2 cups

1 pound softened cream cheese

2 tablespoons half-and-half or milk

2 tablespoons minced fresh parsley

1 tablespoon minced fresh marjoram

1 tablespoon minced fresh savory

2 garlic cloves, finely minced

Salt, to taste

Cayenne pepper, to taste

1 teaspoon herb or white-wine vinegar (optional)

In a medium-size bowl, whisk together the cream cheese and half-and-half. Add the herbs, garlic, salt, cayenne, and vinegar, if desired, and whisk to combine. Cover with plastic wrap and chill for at least 2 hours.

Corn Bread Triangles

A homespun (and easy) recipe for corn bread becomes special with the addition of fresh, fragrant herbs. If stone-ground cornmeal is available, the results will be more delicate.

Makes 8 to 10 servings

1¼ cups all-purpose flour

1 cup yellow cornmeal
(preferably stone-ground)

2 tablespoons sugar

2 teaspoons baking powder

1 teaspoon salt

1¼ cups milk

2 teaspoons water

1 large egg

¼ cup vegetable oil

2 teaspoons fines herbes, such
as savory, marjoram, thyme, or parsley

1. Preheat the oven to 375°F. Butter a 15- by 10-inch jelly-roll pan.

2. In a medium-size bowl, combine the flour, cornmeal, sugar, baking powder, and salt. Mix until well blended. Make a well in the center and add the milk, water, egg, and oil. Mix quickly just until blended (do not overmix). Spread the batter into the prepared pan and sprinkle with the herbs.

3. Bake the corn bread for 12 to 13 minutes, just until golden brown.

4. Using a sharp knife, cut the corn bread on the diagonal into 1½-inch-wide strips. Cut the strips into triangles. Serve immediately or wrap in plastic wrap and then aluminum foil and freeze.

Zucchini-Pistachio Bread

For a slightly spicy frosting on this tempting loaf, use brewed black or oolong (semi-fermented) tea instead of water.

Makes 6 to 8 servings

Zucchini-Pistachio Bread

1 ½ cups all-purpose flour

1 ½ teaspoons baking soda

¼ teaspoon ground cinnamon

¾ cup sugar

2 large eggs

½ cup vegetable oil

1 teaspoon vanilla extract

½ teaspoon salt

1 ½ cups grated zucchini, squeezed dry

1 ½ cups shelled and peeled pistachios, lightly toasted

Vanilla-Scented Frosting

1 large egg white

¾ cup sugar

2 ½ tablespoons cold water

⅛ teaspoon cream of tartar

¾ teaspoon light corn syrup

½ teaspoon vanilla extract

TO MAKE THE ZUCCHINI-PISTACHO BREAD

1. Reheat the oven to 350°F. Generously butter a 9- by 5- by 3-inch loaf pan.

2. Sift together the flour, baking soda, and cinnamon into a bowl.

3. In another bowl, whisk together the sugar, eggs, oil, vanilla, and salt. Add to the dry ingredients and stir until combined. Fold in the zucchini and pistachios.

4. Transfer the batter to the prepared pan and bake for 50 to 60 minutes, until a cake tester inserted in the center comes out clean.

5. Let the bread cool in the pan on a wire rack for 10 minutes. Invert onto the wire rack and cool completely.

TO MAKE THE VANILLA-SCENTED FROSTING

6. In the top of a double boiler set over simmering water, combine the egg white, sugar, water, cream of tartar, and corn syrup. Using a hand mixer, beat the mixture for 7 minutes, or until it is thick and fluffy. Beat in the vanilla.

7. Frost the top of the cooled cake. Allow the frosting to set before serving.

Gifts for Tea Lovers

- Tie up a selection of excellent loose teas in little muslin bags, then wrap plaid silk around them. Add polished flea-market spoons or sugar tongs for gleam.

- Personalize a glass jam jar, honey pot, or plate with safe paints. Try a monogram, a line from a poem, or just "Good Morning, Jane."

- Make a tea caddy unique with découpage. Any upright, airtight tin will work well.

- Create a gift basket with a stacked cup and pot for one, along with teatime treats, teas, jams, a floral honey, or decorated sugar cubes.

- Bake big sugar cookies in the shape of teapots and decorate each one differently.

- Create a tea-themed Christmas tree ornament by mounting your needlepoint cup or pot on a stiff backing with a loop.

- Turn plain cotton or linen napkins into personal treasures with your own tea-themed appliqué or embroidery.

Honey Flan

The fragrance of this silken flan wafting from the kitchen will fill the house with just the right festive air for a celebration.

Makes 6 to 8 servings

Honey Flan

1 ⅓ cups sweet white wine, such as Sauternes or late-harvest Riesling

⅔ cup light flavored honey, such as fragrant lavender

1 strip lemon zest

1 sprig pesticide-free lavender or 1 teaspoon dried

5 large eggs

1 large egg yolk

3 tablespoons sugar

Honey-Scented Whipped Cream

1 cup heavy cream

2 tablespoons light flavored honey, such as fragrant lavender

Pesticide-free rose petals, for garnish

TO MAKE THE HONEY FLAN

1. In a medium-size heavy-bottomed saucepan over medium-high heat, combine the wine, honey, lemon zest, and lavender. Bring the mixture to a simmer, stirring constantly. Remove from the heat and cool.

2. Preheat the oven to 350°F.

3. Strain the wine mixture into a medium-size bowl. In a large bowl, gently whisk the eggs and egg yolk together until blended. Gently whisk in the wine mixture.

4. Spread the sugar in the bottom of an 8- by 1½-inch round glass cake dish. Bake the sugar for 15 to 30 minutes, until it melts and turns a medium caramel color. Cool on a wire rack for 5 minutes. Reduce the oven temperature to 325°F.

5. Pour the egg mixture over the caramelized sugar. Bake for 30 to 35 minutes, until just set in the center when gently shaken.

6. Cool the flan on the wire rack to room temperature.

7. Run a small sharp knife around the side of the dish to loosen the flan. Quickly and carefully invert the flan onto a serving dish.

TO MAKE THE HONEY-SCENTED WHIPPED CREAM

8. In the small bowl of an electric mixer, at high speed, beat the cream and honey until soft peaks form.

9. Cut the flan into wedges and serve with a dollop of the whipped cream. Garnish with rose petals.

Orange-Clove Tea

Mingling citrus, tea leaves, and spice in a single mellow drink, this warming holiday tea is the perfect backdrop for a menu that combines the zestiness of garlic, the tartness of sorrel, and the sweetness of honey. For variety's sake, try this recipe with another, lesser-known black tea, Keemun, whose bright red liquor lends itself to holiday celebrations. Lapsang souchong, a slightly smoky black tea, would be another fine choice for this menu, as it complements spicy foods and cheese. Use cinnamon sticks as stirrers.

Makes 6 servings

½ orange, sliced

Whole cloves

6 cups hot brewed orange pekoe tea

Cut each orange slice in half (so each piece is a semicircle) and stud the skin side with several whole cloves. Pour the tea into 6 cups. Float a cloved orange slice in each cup when serving. For extra flavor, add two orange slices to the pot while it is brewing.

Sweet Pairings

Matching the flavors of teas to foods can be a great taste adventure, and not just for the connoisseur. Whether you're serving dessert after an extensive meal or afternoon teatime sweets, consider trying these pairings.

With fruit-based desserts: Dragon Well, a Chinese green tea, or jasmine or Keemun, both oolongs, would be perfect with cherry pie, as shown opposite, or other fruit pies, cobblers, or tarts.

With creamy or chocolate desserts: A hearty black tea, such as gold-tipped Assam from India or Earl Grey; Matcha, a bright Japanese green tea; or peppermint tea would all be delightful paired with a flourless chocolate cake or an assortment of chocolate truffles.

For a complete (not to mention sublime) menu for a tea party featuring sweets, see page 157.

*If you are cold, tea will warm you;
if you are too heated, it will cool you;
if you are depressed, it will cheer you;
if you are excited, it will calm you.*

—William E. Gladstone

More *Delightful* *Recipes* for *Teas* and *Treats*

Delight friends and family with our teatime recipes: home-brewed teas, sandwiches and other savory bites, quick breads, cookies, cakes, tarts, and then some. With this selection of irresistible recipes at your fingertips, you can put together casual teatime menus on the fly or take your time planning an extra-special tea party. Sprinkled throughout, you'll find charming menu ideas (and words of tea wisdom) to inspire you.

Opposite: Tea and cookies were made for each other.
For a sweet selection of cookie recipes, see page 155.

I believe it is customary in good society to take some slight refreshment at five o'clock.

—Oscar Wilde, *The Importance of Being Earnest*

Traditional Teatime Menus

One of the most delightful aspects of the Victorian tea is its balance of sweet and savory. The British are well known for their love of mustard, vinegar, and herbs, which in the form of savories are just the thing to accompany the ultra-rich sweets. It is wonderful to rely on tradition when it comes to menu choices. Cream cakes, warm scones, madeleines, jam tarts, and tiny sandwiches with slivered ham are all in the Victorian mode, made from recipes that cannot be improved upon. A few continental liberties can be taken, such as salmon mousse or fancy puff pastries, but if you choose you can stay truly British and never run out of new menu ideas, for the variety is both prolific and delicious.

Above and opposite: Tea and a three-tiered silver cake server create instant Old World ambience.

Tea sandwiches are little bites of fresh flavors that never overwhelm the tea itself. Classics are thinly sliced cucumbers and watercress. The English loaf is never too sweet, square, flat and topped with a small crumb and close texture. Its crusts are always removed. (They can be toasted and used for bread crumbs.) Butter is sweet, not salted, and often delicately flavored with herbs like basil or sage.

When you plan your menu, take the season into consideration. This will dictate whether you will serve hot or iced tea, and the kinds of fruits you can use fresh in recipes like Country Peach and Plum Tart or Blackberry Tarts. A cold and snowy February inspired Black Walnut Linzer Hearts and piping hot Currant Scones with Smoked Turkey. Select seasonal ingredients whenever possible. All produce tastes superior when it is grown close to home rather than halfway around the world.

A Word about Ingredients

As well as perfectly ripe seasonal fruits and berries, we suggest choosing only the finest ingredients for all these teatime treats. When developing the recipes, we used large grade A eggs, unsalted butter, and pure vanilla extract. If a recipe calls for already baked bread, buy the best at a local bakery or market. Buy nuts in the shells from specialty markets or natural food stores; these are fresher than those in the cellophane-wrapped

packets sold in supermarkets. We recommend freshly squeezed lemon juice rather than bottled, and fresh herbs when possible. In our recipes, "sugar" always means granulated sugar unless specified otherwise.

Bake the sweets and make the savory dishes as close to serving time as possible. In the recipes, we have provided storing information when appropriate. You can make tea sandwiches, for instance, several hours before tea, keeping them fresh under a damp tea towel. Many cakes and quick breads mellow and actually taste better if made a day or so ahead of time. Scones and muffins are best served as soon after baking as possible, and pancakes and waffles do not tolerate storage.

Above: For best results, make your tea sandwiches with fresh herbs and bread from a good local bakery or farmer's market.

A WORD ABOUT INGREDIENTS

Brewing the Perfect Pot of Tea

Much has been written about brewing tea. The consensus is that a good pot of tea requires three elements: pure water (the softer the better), boiling water, and loose tea (although tea bags, in a pinch, will do!).

To begin, put cold water on to boil in the kettle (this of course should be metal). Cold, running water (not iced) is fully oxygenated and better for tea. If your tap water is very hard or poor-tasting, use bottled water. Fill a porcelain teapot with hot tap water and let it sit to warm up while the kettle boils. Just before the water reaches the boil, empty the teapot, dry it, and add the tea. The rule of thumb is one heaping teaspoon of tea for each cup, and then one more "for the pot." If you are using tea bags, use one for each serving and one more for the pot.

Set the teapot next to the stove and the moment the water boils, pour it over the tea. It is important that the water be boiling as fully as possible; if you carry the teakettle across the room, the water may drop a degree or two in the few seconds this journey may take. Equally important is that the water not boil too long. If it has been boiling for several minutes or more, not only will you lose much of it to steam, but the water will lose oxygen and the tea will not taste as good.

Let the tea steep for three to five minutes. Stir it once during steeping to distribute the essential oils. Steeping draws the tannin from the leaves; too much steeping will result in bitter tea. The strength of the tea depends as much on the amount used as on the steeping time. Finally, strain the tea into another warm teapot or directly into cups for serving.

Teas

Throughout this section you'll find recipes for hot teas, iced teas, tea-based punches, and even a rosehip tea cooler. For additional options, see the following tea recipes within the party menus:

Mint Tea

The smoky flavor of China tea is perfectly complemented by bits of fresh mint leaves. Add sugar, if you desire, and lemon slices and mint sprigs for a bit more flavor and color.

Makes 4 servings

3 teaspoons China tea

¼ cup chopped fresh mint

3½ to 4 cups boiling water

4 lemon slices and mint sprigs

4 to 5 teaspoons sugar, optional

1. Warm a teapot and teacups with hot water. Drain and dry them.

2. Combine the tea leaves and chopped mint in the teapot. Add the boiling water. Cover with a tea towel or tea cozy and steep for 5 minutes.

3. Stir and strain into the hot cups, and garnish with lemon slices and mint sprigs. Serve right away, with or without the sugar.

Iced Lemon-Mint Tea

Lemon and mint are a classic combination. Try the tea iced with Lime Wafers (page 158) or Lemon Tea Bread (page 139).

Makes 6 to 8 servings

2 quarts water

2 tablespoons lemon tea

2 tablespoons mint tea

6 to 8 lemon slices

1. In a large saucepan, bring the water to a full boil. Add the lemon and mint teas, either loose or in a fine mesh infuser. Cover and let the tea stand for 5 minutes.

2. Strain and cool to room temperature.

3. Serve the tea over ice, garnished with the lemon slices.

Cozy Tea for Two

Currant and Pecan Scones
Grilled Marmalade Fingers
Meringue Kisses
Lemon Ginger Pound Cake
Berry-Flavored Honey
Orange-Spice Tea

Iced Orange-Spice Tea

Fragrant orange-pekoe tea is enhanced when it is infused with a cinnamon stick and a pod of star anise, which tastes like licorice.

Makes 6 to 8 servings

2 quarts water

8 teaspoons loose orange-pekoe tea

½ cup sugar

1 stick cinnamon

1 pod star anise

6 to 8 quartered orange slices

1. In a large saucepan, bring the water to a full boil. Add the tea, sugar, cinnamon, and star anise. Cover and let the tea stand for 5 minutes.

2. Strain and cool to room temperature.

3. Serve the tea over ice, garnished with the orange slices.

Iced Ginger-Pear Delight

Serving ginger-flavored sweets was common in Victorian times. Here, ginger is steeped in boiling water to yield a mildly flavored tea that blends nicely with rich fruit nectar.

Makes 5 servings

2 tablespoons thinly sliced fresh ginger

½ cup boiling water

2 cups pear, peach, or apricot nectar

2 cups club soda, chilled

5 pear, peach, or apricot slices, dipped in freshly squeezed lemon juice

1. Put the ginger in a small teapot or bowl. Pour the boiling water over it and let it steep, covered, for about 10 minutes, or until cool. Strain and mix the cooled ginger liquid with the fruit nectar.

2. For each serving, pour ½ cup of the ginger-nectar mixture over ice in glass. Add about ⅓ cup of chilled club soda. Stir gently and garnish with the sliced fruit.

Surely everyone is aware of the divine pleasures which attend a wintry fireside: candles at four o'clock, warm hearth rugs, tea, a fair tea-maker, shutters closed, curtains flowing in ample draperies to the floor, whilst the wind and rain are raging audibly without.

—Thomas De Quincey

Lovers' Tea

This tea is a personal blend to make and store in a tin. Bring it out when the occasion merits something special. For a charming presentation, serve in dainty teacups and decorate with floating rose petals. The rose petals may be from the dozen long-stems delivered that afternoon, or perhaps they were recently cut from rose bushes in the garden. (Just be sure they are pesticide free.)

 *Makes 16 to 20 servings*

1 cup loose jasmine tea leaves

1 tablespoon dried lavender flowers

1 teaspoon dried marjoram

¼ cup dried rose petals

32 to 40 fresh, pesticide-free rose petals (2 for each cup)

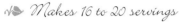 Lovers' Tea

TO MAKE THE DRIED TEA MIXTURE

1. In a medium bowl, combine the tea leaves, lavender flowers, marjoram, and rose petals.

2. Transfer the mixture to a container with a tight-fitting lid and store it in a cool, dark place.

TO MAKE THE TEA

1. Warm a teapot and teacups with hot water. Drain and dry them.

2. For each cup of tea, put 1 tablespoon of the tea mixture and ¾ cup boiling water into the teapot. Cover with a tea towel or tea cozy and steep for 5 minutes.

3. Stir the tea and strain it into the cups.

4. Remove the bitter white heel from each rose petal. Crush the petals slightly to release their flavor and then gently float 2 petals on the surface of each cup of tea. Serve right away.

126

Iced Lavender and Lime Tea

We can't imagine a more refreshing iced summer drink than this blend of fragrant lavender and tangy lime. And it looks so pretty poured into tall, frosty glasses.

Makes 5 servings

3 tablespoons crushed fresh lavender flowers, or 1 tablespoon dried lavender flowers

1 cup boiling water

1 6-ounce can frozen limeade concentrate

5 lavender flower sprigs

1. Place the lavender flowers in a small teapot or bowl. Pour the boiling water over the flowers. Steep, covered, for at least 10 minutes, or until cool.

2. While the tea is cooling, prepare the limeade according to the package directions.

3. Stir and strain the tea into the limeade. Serve over ice, with the flower sprigs.

Rosy Yogurt Cooler

This frothy berry-filled yogurt shake will appeal to those who are not overly fond of plain tea. Depending on the size of your blender, you may have to make this recipe in several batches.

Makes 4 servings

2 rosehip tea bags

2 cups boiling water

2 cups plain lowfat yogurt

1 cup sliced strawberries, blueberries, or raspberries, plus additional, for garnish

3 tablespoons honey

1. Put the rosehip tea bags in a small teapot or bowl. Pour the boiling water over them and let them steep, covered, for about 10 minutes. Remove the tea bags.

2. Put the yogurt, berries, and honey in a blender. Blend until smooth.

3. Add the tea to the yogurt mixture. Blend until smooth.

4. Serve over ice, with whole berries.

And is there honey still for tea?

—Rupert Brooke, *The Old Vicarage, Grantchester*

Double Lemon Punch

Gently flavored with lemon-verbena leaves or lemon tea, this ginger ale–based punch is a pretty addition to the tea table. Children will like it, too, and guests will be charmed by the flowery ice cubes. Be sure to make some extra ice cubes to replenish the punch.

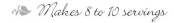 *Makes 8 to 10 servings*

Floral Ice

16 to 24 small edible flowers such as borage, sage, lavender, rose petals, or rose buds, or 10 to 14 large edible flowers such as calendula or nasturtium

Punch

½ cup fresh lemon-verbena leaves, or 3 tablespoons dried leaves, or 2 lemon tea bags

2 cups boiling water

2 cups black tea, cooled

Juice of 2 lemons

1 quart ginger ale, chilled

 Double Lemon Punch

TO MAKE THE FLORAL ICE

1. Gently wash the flowers and place 1 or 2 small ones in each compartment of an ice tray. Add water in a soft stream and freeze.

2. Or, for a larger block of ice, use an 8- or 9-inch cake pan. Scatter the large flowers, blossom side down in the cake pan, or mix them with some smaller blooms. Add ⅛ inch of cold water. Freeze until firm, about 1 hour. Fill the cake pan almost full with cold water. Freeze for 5 hours or until frozen. Dip the pan in hot water to loosen the ice block.

TO MAKE AND SERVE THE PUNCH

1. Place the lemon-verbena leaves or lemon tea bags in a small teapot or bowl. Pour boiling water over them and let the mixture steep, covered, for at least 10 minutes. Strain or remove the tea bags.

2. In a large punch bowl, mix the cooled lemon tea, cooled black tea, and lemon juice. Cover and refrigerate until serving time, or for at least 30 minutes.

3. Just before serving, add the ginger ale. Stir gently to mix. Float the floral ice in the punch.

White Winter Champagne Punch

This is an elegant punch for a fancy tea. The wine and port combine with bubbling champagne, to be ladled from a crystal punch bowl into the pretty sugar-iced glasses. Lemon-verbena gives off a pleasing lemon scent and may be used to make a wreath to encircle the punch bowl.

Makes 12 to 15 servings

Lemon-Verbena Sugar

1 cup lemon-verbena leaves

2 cups superfine sugar

Punch

2 cups lemon-flavored mineral water

1 cup superfine sugar

½ cup lemon-verbena leaves

1 (750 ml) bottle white burgundy, chilled

1 (750 ml) bottle white port, chilled

3 (750 ml) bottles brut champagne, chilled

3 lemons, for glasses

12 to 15 lemon-verbena leaves

TO PREPARE THE SUGAR

From a week to a month ahead, mix the lemon-verbena leaves with the sugar. Store in a tightly covered container, shaking occasionally to mix.

TO MAKE THE PUNCH

1. The day before serving, boil the mineral water and superfine sugar for 5 minutes to make a simple syrup. Remove from the heat and make an infusion by adding the lemon-verbena leaves. Cover and let the infusion sit at room temperature overnight.

2. Just before serving, mix the infusion with the chilled burgundy and port in a punch bowl. Slowly pour the chilled champagne down the side of the bowl and stir.

TO PREPARE THE GLASSES AND SERVE

1. Cut the lemons into wedges. Run the lemon wedges over the inside of saucer-shaped champagne glasses and ½-inch of the outside rim of each glass.

2. In a shallow bowl, pie plate, or saucer, spoon the lemon-verbena sugar so that it is about an inch deep. Dip the lemon-moistened rim of each glass in the sugar. Sprinkle some into the glass and swirl to coat. Repeat for each glass.

3. Chill the glasses in the refrigerator for at least 30 minutes, or in the freezer for at least 15 minutes, or until serving time.

4. When it is time to serve, ladle the punch into the sugar-frosted glasses and garnish with lemon-verbena leaves.

Love and scandal are the best sweeteners of tea.

—Henry Fielding, *Love in Several Masques*

My experience. . . convinced me that tea was better than brandy.

—Theodore Roosevelt

Savories

Throughout this section, you'll find recipes for tea sandwiches and other savory morsels. For additional options, see the following recipes within the party menus:

Smoked Salmon Canapés, page 102

Goat Cheese Toasts with Pink Peppercorns, page 93

Stilton, Pear, and Watercress Savory Toasts, page 61

Sorrel, Leek, and Mushroom Tart, page 110

Currant Scones with Smoked Turkey, page 68

Cucumber-Basil Tea Sandwiches, page 94

Tomato and Goat Cheese Sandwiches, page 62

Watercress and Nasturtium Sandwiches, page 102

Above and opposite: Tea sandwiches should feature very fine white bread and light fillings.

Watercress Sandwiches

As the custom of taking afternoon tea gained in popularity during the nineteenth century, the array of delicate morsels served with the hot drink got more elaborate. Soon sweets accompanied the buttered bread and muffins, and then came tea sandwiches made from very fine white bread and light-tasting ingredients such as watercress, tomatoes, cucumbers, and chopped egg. If you make tea sandwiches ahead of time, keep them covered with a damp, well-wrung tea towel so they won't dry out.

Makes 12 sandwiches

Ham-Watercress Sandwiches

2 thin slices white bread, crusts removed

2 tablespoons cream cheese with chives, softened

2 thin slices baked ham

1/3 cup small watercress sprigs, thick stems removed

12 orange sections

2 teaspoons minced red onion

1. Spread the slices of bread with the cream cheese.

2. Trim the ham to fit the slices of bread. Layer the ham and watercress on the bread. Using a serrated knife, cut the sandwich in half diagonally.

3. Just before serving, garnish the sandwiches with orange sections and sprinkle with red onion.

Chicken-Watercress Sandwiches

2 thin slices white bread, crusts removed

2 tablespoons cream cheese with chives, softened

4 thin slices cooked chicken breast

1/3 cup small watercress sprigs, thick stems removed

12 thick cucumber slices

4 strips pimiento

1. Spread the slices of bread with the cream cheese.

2. Trim the chicken to fit the slices of bread. Layer the chicken and watercress on the bread. Using a serrated knife, cut the sandwich in half diagonally.

3. Just before serving, garnish the sandwiches with cucumber and pimiento.

Bacon-Watercress Sandwiches

2 thin slices white bread, crusts removed

2 tablespoons cream cheese with chives, softened

2 slices bacon, cooked and crumbled

1/3 cup small watercress sprigs, thick stems removed

4 avocado slices, brushed with lemon juice

Paprika

1. Spread the slices of bread with the cream cheese.

2. Top the bread with bacon and watercress. Using a serrated knife, cut the sandwich in half diagonally.

3. Just before serving, garnish the sandwiches with avocado slices and sprinkle with paprika.

Herbed Cream Cheese Sandwiches

Cream cheese with herbs fresh from your own garden or the local market makes a fine tea sandwich. You can prepare the cream cheese mixture several hours ahead, but let it come to room temperature before spreading it on the bread.

Makes 16 sandwiches

1 cup (8 ounces) cream cheese, softened

½ cup lightly packed finely chopped fresh herb leaves such as parsley, watercress, basil, chervil, or chives, by themselves or in any combination

1 tablespoon freshly squeezed lemon juice

Dash of bottled hot pepper sauce

8 slices firm-textured wheat bread, crusts removed

Paprika

1. In a small mixing bowl, combine the cream cheese, herbs, lemon juice, and hot pepper sauce.

2. Spread about 2 tablespoons of the mixture on each slice of bread. Sprinkle with paprika.

3. Put the slices together to make 4 sandwiches. Using a serrated knife, cut them diagonally into quarters.

Cucumber Sandwiches with Mint Butter

Simple and elegant, cucumber sandwiches are the stuff of teatime. With a handful of mint leaves added to the butter, these are especially tasty. Burnet leaves, commonly found in Europe and Asia, are cultivated here for their young, tender leaves, which taste a little like cucumber. As such, they are perfect for embellishing a plateful of delicate sandwiches. Look for them in your local produce market.

Makes 8 sandwiches

¼ cup (½ stick) butter, softened

2 tablespoons fresh mint leaves, chopped

8 very thin slices white bread, crusts removed

½ large cucumber, peeled and thinly sliced

Burnet sprigs and ripe black olives (optional)

1. In a small bowl, combine the butter and mint.

2. Spread the mint butter on the bread slices. Lay the cucumber on 4 of the slices and top with the remaining bread to make 4 sandwiches. Cut them in half diagonally.

3. Just before serving, garnish the sandwiches with burnet sprigs and olives, if desired.

 Cucumber Sandwiches with Mint Butter

Salmon Mousse

The light, delicate flavor of these individual mousses is extremely appropriate for late-afternoon tea. If the mousses do not unmold easily, dip them into a bowl of very hot water for just a few seconds.

🐟 *Makes 10 servings*

1 envelope unflavored gelatin

½ cup cold water

½ cup boiling water

½ cup mayonnaise

1 tablespoon grated onion

1 tablespoon freshly squeezed lemon juice

1 teaspoon salt

½ teaspoon paprika

½ teaspoon bottled hot pepper sauce

2 cups drained, flaked salmon

½ cup heavy cream

1. In a medium bowl, sprinkle the gelatin over the cold water. Let it stand for 5 minutes, until it is softened. Add the boiling water and stir until the gelatin dissolves. Let it cool to room temperature.

2. Whisk the mayonnaise, onion, lemon juice, salt, paprika, and hot pepper sauce into the gelatin. Mix well. Cover the bowl and refrigerate for 30 to 60 minutes, or until the mixture is the consistency of unbeaten egg whites.

3. Butter ten ⅓-cup molds.

4. Remove the mixture from the refrigerator and stir in the salmon. Beat well with an electric mixer set at medium speed.

5. In a small bowl, whip the cream until soft peaks form. Fold the whipped cream into the salmon mixture. Fill each of the prepared molds. Cover and refrigerate until set, at least 4 hours.

6. To serve, loosen the edges of the molds with a knife. Invert the molds on a serving plate and, gently shaking each one, lift it off the mousse.

Spinach-Cheese Tartlets

The filling for these dainty tartlets is quick and simple to make. The pastry shells, which take a little longer to prepare, may be made ahead of time and stored in the freezer.

🐟 *Makes 30 to 32 tartlets*

Pastry

½ cup (1 stick) cold butter, cut into pieces

6 tablespoons lard

2½ cups all-purpose flour

4 to 6 tablespoons ice water

Filling

4 eggs

1½ cups (12 ounces) cottage cheese

1 small onion, finely chopped

2 garlic cloves, minced

1 10-ounce package frozen chopped spinach, thawed

1 cup shredded Monterey jack cheese

½ cup freshly grated Parmesan cheese

½ teaspoon salt

TO MAKE THE PASTRY

1. In a large bowl, cut the butter and lard into the flour with a pastry blender or 2 knives until the mixture resembles coarse crumbs. Sprinkle the ice water over the mixture, 1 tablespoon at a time, stirring with a fork until the pastry is well blended and gathers into a ball. Sprinkle the dough with a little flour. Wrap it in plastic and refrigerate at least 1 hour.

2. Divide the chilled dough into 2 portions. Roll one portion out onto a lightly floured work surface into a circle about $\frac{1}{8}$ inch thick. Cut out pieces to fit onto $2\frac{1}{2}$- to 3-inch tartlet pans. Gently press the pieces of dough into the pans and prick them on the bottom with a fork. Repeat with the second portion of dough. Put the pans on a baking sheet and place them in the freezer for about 15 minutes, or until the dough is firm.

3. Preheat the oven to 375°F. Cut small squares of foil, each about 3 inches square, for each tartlet.

4. Remove the pans from the freezer. Line the pastry with the foil squares, shiny side down, and fill the foil with dried beans, rice, or pastry weights to keep the pastry flat during baking.

5. Bake the pastry shells 12 to 15 minutes, or until the foil lifts out of the shells easily. Remove the foil and weights from the shells. Continue baking the shells 8 to 10 minutes, or until the pastry is very lightly browned and firm. Cool the shells completely, about 45 minutes, in the pans.

6. Remove the cooled shells from the pans. They may be stored in the refrigerator in a tightly closed container for a few days or in the freezer for several weeks.

TO MAKE THE TARTLETS

1. Preheat the oven to 375°F. In a medium bowl, beat the eggs. Add the cottage cheese, onion, and garlic and mix well.

2. In a sieve, press the water out of the spinach. Add the spinach, cheeses, and salt to the egg mixture. Stir until well mixed.

3. Fill each baked pastry shell with about 2 tablespoons of filling.

4. Put the shells on baking sheets and bake for 20 to 22 minutes, or until they are puffed and golden on top. Serve hot.

Putting on the Ritz

Salmon Mousse
Goat Cheese Toasts with Pink Peppercorns
Watercress and Nasturtium Sandwiches
White Grape Tart
Meringue Kisses
White Winter Champagne Punch

I always fear that creation will expire before teatime.

—Sydney Smith

Breads

Throughout this section, you'll find recipes for quick breads, muffins, biscuits, scones, and more. For still more options, see the following recipes within the party menus:

Above and oppo-site: Hot buttered scones and a cup of tea will always be a satisfying match.

Sage Bread

It is said that sage, an herb long popular in the Mediterranean countries of Europe, brings prosperity and good health to all who grow it. Long ago the Dutch dried sage leaves, much as tea is dried, and traded it with the Chinese for China tea. Today, adding sage to a simple loaf such as this one gives the bread a strong, true flavor that enhances a good cup of tea.

✍ *Makes one 9-inch loaf*

½ cup milk

2 tablespoons chopped fresh sage, or 1 tablespoon dried sage

2 cups all-purpose flour

1 tablespoon baking powder

1 teaspoon salt

½ cup (1 stick) butter, softened

½ cup sugar

2 eggs

1. Preheat the oven to 350°F. Butter and flour a 9- by 5- by 3-inch loaf pan.

2. In a small saucepan, combine the milk and sage, and bring almost to a boil over medium heat. Remove the milk mixture from the heat and let it stand until cool.

3. In a medium bowl, stir together the flour, baking powder, and salt. Set aside.

4. In the medium bowl of an electric mixer, beat the butter at medium speed to soften. Gradually add the sugar and continue beating until the mixture is light and fluffy, scraping the sides of the bowl often. Add the eggs, one at a time, beating well after each addition.

5. Strain the milk to remove the sage, if desired. If you do not strain it, the bread will have a more pronounced sage flavor.

6. Add the flour mixture and milk alternately to the butter mixture, stirring well with a wooden spoon after each addition. Spread the batter evenly in the prepared pan.

7. Bake the bread for 50 to 60 minutes, or until a toothpick inserted in center of the loaf comes out clean.

8. Cool the bread in the pan on a wire rack for 10 minutes. Then remove the bread from the pan to cool on the rack.

A Classic English Tea

Cucumber Sandwiches with Mint Butter

Watercress Sandwiches

Salmon Mousse

Madeleines

Lemon Bread

Ginger-Flavored Honey

Lily of the Valley Cake

Mint Tea

Lemon Tea Bread

Because this bread is made with lemonade, lemon zest, and lemon extract, the flavor is wonderfully intense. We suggest making the lemonade for the bread from frozen concentrate rather than relying on pre-mixed lemonade or that from fresh lemons. The sweet loaf slices easily and requires no accompaniment other than a nice cup of tea.

Makes one 9-inch loaf

2 cups all-purpose flour

1 tablespoon baking powder

¼ teaspoon salt

½ cup (1 stick) butter, softened

1 cup sugar

2 eggs

grated zest of 1 lemon

1 teaspoon lemon extract

¾ cup lemonade

1. Preheat the oven to 350°F. Butter and flour a 9- by 5- by 3-inch loaf pan. Line the bottom of the pan with wax paper. Butter and flour the wax paper. Shake out excess flour.

2. In a medium bowl, thoroughly stir together the flour, baking powder, and salt.

3. In the medium bowl of an electric mixer, beat the butter and sugar at medium speed until the mixture is light and fluffy, scraping the sides of the bowl often. Add the eggs, one at a time, beating well after each addition.

4. Add the lemon zest and lemon extract. With the mixer set at low speed, add the dry ingredients alternately with the lemonade, and mix just until blended. Spread the batter evenly in the prepared pan.

5. Bake for 60 to 65 minutes, or until a toothpick inserted in the center of the loaf comes out clean.

6. Cool the bread in the pan on a wire rack for 10 minutes. Then remove from the pan, peel off the wax paper, and let the bread cool completely on the rack.

If one would merely slake his thirst, then he can drink rice and water. Should melancholy, sadness, or anger strike, he can turn to drink. But if one would dispel an evening's unproductive lassitude, the meaning of "drink" is tea.

—Lu Yu, *The Classic of Tea*

Lemon Thyme Bread

Lemon thyme has a noticeable and extremely pleasant lemony tang. In this quick loaf, it not only adds bright lemon flavor, but flecks the crumb with pretty green accents.

Makes one 9-inch loaf

2 cups all-purpose flour

2 teaspoons baking powder

¼ teaspoon salt

6 tablespoons (¾ stick) butter, softened

1 cup sugar

2 eggs

1 tablespoons grated lemon zest

2 tablespoons freshly squeezed lemon juice

2 tablespoons finely chopped lemon thyme

⅔ cup milk

2 tablespoons freshly squeezed lemon juice, for glazing

½ cup sifted confectioners' sugar for glazing

1. Preheat the oven to 350°F. Butter and flour a 9- by 5- by 3-inch loaf pan.

2. In a medium bowl, sift together the flour, baking powder, and salt. Set aside.

3. In the medium bowl of an electric mixer, beat the butter and sugar at medium speed until the mixture is light and fluffy, scraping the sides of the bowl often. Add the eggs, one at a time, beating well after each addition.

4. Beat in the lemon zest, lemon juice, and lemon thyme. With the mixer at low speed, add the dry ingredients alternately with the milk, and mix until just blended. Spread the batter in the prepared pan.

5. Bake for 55 to 60 minutes, or until a toothpick inserted in the center of the loaf comes out clean. Cool the baked bread in the pan on a wire rack for 10 minutes.

6. While the bread is cooling, make a glaze. In a small bowl, mix the lemon juice and enough confectioners' sugar for a thin, pourable consistency.

7. Turn the bread out onto a wire rack positioned over a sheet of paper. Slowly pour the glaze over the bread.

 Lemon Thyme Bread

Milk and Honey Bread with Honey Butter

Few cups of tea are more comforting than those sweetened with a little milk and honey—and nothing tastes better with tea than a thick slice of sweet honey bread, rich with its own honey butter. Serve this satisfying combination when the occasion calls for something warm and soothing.

Makes one 9-inch loaf

1 cup milk

½ cup honey

3 tablespoons butter, melted

2½ cups all-purpose flour

½ cup sugar

1 tablespoon baking powder

1 teaspoon salt

¾ cup chopped pecans

1 egg

Honey Butter

½ cup (1 stick) butter, softened

½ cup honey

2 tablespoons heavy cream

TO MAKE THE BREAD

1. Preheat the oven to 375°F. Butter a 9- by 5- by 3-inch loaf pan.

2. In a medium saucepan, combine the milk and honey. Stir over medium heat until the honey is dissolved. Stir in the melted butter. Set aside to cool.

3. In a large bowl, sift together the flour, sugar, baking powder and salt. Add the pecans and toss to mix. Set the mixture aside.

4. Pour the cooled milk mixture into the large bowl of an electric mixer and beat in the egg. When it is well blended, add the flour mixture. With the mixer at medium speed, beat just until the ingredients are blended. Spread the batter evenly in the prepared pan.

5. Turn down the oven to 350°F and bake the bread for 65 to 70 minutes, or until a toothpick inserted in the center of the loaf comes out clean.

6. Cool the bread in the pan on a wire rack for 10 minutes. Remove it from the pan and let it cool completely on the rack.

TO MAKE THE BUTTER

1. In the medium bowl of an electric mixer, beat the butter at medium speed to soften. Beat in the honey until blended.

2. Gradually beat in the cream until the mixture is smooth and creamy. Serve at room temperature.

An After-School Tea

Milk and Honey Bread with Honey Butter
Pumpkin Biscuits
Dreamy Almond Cookies
Gingerbread Girls and Boys
Blackberry Jam Cake
Vanilla Milk Tea
Double Lemon Punch

Currant and Pecan Scones

Scones are as expected on the tea table as the teapot itself. Quintessential examples are these, made with currants and pecans. Traditional companions for scones are some sweet butter, or a dollop of Devonshire or softly beaten cream.

Makes 24 scones

3½ cups all-purpose flour

2 teaspoons baking soda

½ teaspoon salt

½ cup (1 stick) butter, softened

1 cup dried currants or chopped raisins

½ cup finely chopped pecans

1½ cups half-and-half

2 tablespoons sugar

1 teaspoon ground cinnamon

1. Preheat the oven to 400°F. Butter 2 baking sheets.

2. In a large bowl, stir together the flour, baking soda, and salt. With 2 knives or a pastry blender, cut the butter into the flour mixture until it resembles coarse crumbs. Stir in the fruit and the pecans. Make a well in the center of the mixture and add the half-and-half. Stir gently with a fork to make a soft, cohesive dough.

3. Turn the dough out onto a well-floured surface and knead it 10 to 12 times. Roll the dough into a ¼-inch thickness. Cut the dough into rounds using a 2-inch floured biscuit cutter or an upturned floured glass.

4. In a small bowl, combine the sugar and cinnamon. Arrange the scones, ½ inch apart on the prepared baking sheets. Sprinkle the scones with the sugar mixture.

5. Bake the scones for 10 to 12 minutes, or until they are golden brown. Serve warm.

Currant and Pecan Scones

Pumpkin Biscuits

Whole-wheat flour and pumpkin puree produce substantial biscuits that taste just right with a hearty tea.

Makes about 16 biscuits

1 cup all-purpose flour

1 cup whole-wheat pastry flour

2 tablespoons packed dark-brown sugar

1 tablespoon baking powder

1 teaspoon pumpkin-pie spice

1 teaspoon salt

½ cup (1 stick) cold butter, cut into 8 pieces

1 8-ounce can pumpkin puree, or 1 cup fresh pumpkin, cooked and mashed

2 tablespoons heavy cream

Pumpkin Biscuits

1. Preheat the oven to 450°F.

2. In a food processor, combine both flours, the brown sugar, baking powder, pumpkin-pie spice, and salt. Process until the mixture is blended.

3. Distribute the butter evenly over the flour mixture in the processor. Pulse the processor on and off until the butter is the size of peas.

4. Spoon the pumpkin puree evenly over the flour mixture, still in the bowl of the processor. Process until the dough begins to come together but has not yet formed a ball. The dough should be soft. Do not overprocess it or the biscuits will be tough.

5. On a lightly floured board, pat out the dough with floured fingers to make a 9-inch-diameter circle about ½ inch thick. With a floured 2-inch biscuit cutter or upturned glass, cut out biscuits.

6. Place the biscuit rounds on an unbuttered baking sheet. Brush each lightly with cream. With a fork, prick the top of each biscuit twice.

7. Bake for 12 to 14 minutes, or until the biscuits are lightly browned. Serve warm.

Heavenly Pancakes

These sweet little pancakes are delicious simply dressed with a sprinkling of confectioners' sugar and a squeeze of lemon juice, then drizzled with Blackberry Syrup (page 151) or spread with Spiced Blackberry Jam (page 152). Whatever your pleasure, make them just before serving time so that they come to the table piping hot and fresh off the griddle.

Makes fifty to sixty 2½-inch pancakes

4 eggs

5 tablespoons cake flour

3 tablespoons sugar

1 teaspoon baking soda

½ teaspoon salt

2 cups sour cream

Butter or vegetable oil

1. Place the eggs in a blender or a food processor. Add the flour, sugar, baking soda, and salt, and blend or process until the mixture is smooth.

2. Spoon in the sour cream and process again until smooth.

3. Heat a griddle or a heavy skillet brushed with butter or vegetable oil. When it is hot, drop a 1-tablespoon measure of batter onto the griddle for each 2½-inch round. (Do not attempt to make larger hotcakes; they will be too fragile to turn.)

4. Cook each one for 40 to 50 seconds, until a few bubbles appear on top, and then carefully turn and cook the other side of each for 20 to 30 seconds, until the pancakes are golden brown. Serve immediately, if possible, or keep the pancakes warm by covering them with foil and putting them in the oven set at a low temperature while you cook the remaining batter.

A Perfect Brunch

Heavenly Pancakes

Lemon Thyme Bread

Blackberry Muffin Miniatures

Raised Waffles

Blackberry Syrup

Strawberry Butter

Orange Honey

Mint Tea

The mere clink of cups and saucers turns the mind to happy repose.

—George Gissie

Spreads

Throughout this section, you'll find recipes for flavored butters, honeys, jams, and even traditional sauces for topping puddings. For additional options, see the following recipes within the party menus:

Above: Consider dressing up ramekins of honey butter with nasturtium, or other small edible flowers.

Ginger-Flavored Honey

Once the spice trade began between Europe and the Orient, ginger was one of the most prized commodities and found its way into the cooking of England and eventually to America. It remains popular today on both sides of the Atlantic. We particularly enjoy the spicy flavor of ginger combined with the natural sweetness of the honey. If the candied ginger is too sticky to chop easily, chill it a bit first.

Makes 2½ cups

2 cups (16 ounces) light-colored honey

½ cup chopped candied ginger

In a small saucepan, stir the honey over medium heat until warmed through. Stir in the ginger. Pour the honey into a heatproof jar and cover. Let the mixture cool to room temperature before serving.

Herb-Flavored Honey

This lightly scented honey is a fine addition to any tea tray and tastes very good indeed with Lemon Tea Bread (page 139) or Sage Bread (page 138). It looks jewel-like served in cut glass or even in a recycled glass jar.

Makes 2 cups

2 cups (16 ounces) light-colored honey

6 to 7 sprigs fresh herbs such as lavender, mint, thyme, or rosemary

In a small saucepan, stir the honey over medium heat until warmed through. Put the herb sprigs or the chopped leaves of the herbs in a heatproof jar and pour the honey over them. Cool to room temperature. Cover tightly and let the honey stand for a day or two before serving.

 Herb-Flavored Honey

Orange Honey

Honey infused with fragrant orange zest is delicious with full-flavored breads. For the best results, select a robust honey such as clover or alfalfa, rather than a more delicate variety such as raspberry or blueberry. Pale golden specialty honeys, made by bees pollinating raspberry and blueberry bushes, taste light and delicious but they are not as full-bodied as clover or alfalfa honey.

Makes 2 cups

2 cups (8 ounces) honey
Grated zest of 1 orange

In a small saucepan, stir the honey over medium heat until warmed through. Stir in the orange zest. Pour the honey into a heatproof jar and cover. Let the mixture cool to room temperature before serving.

Berry-Flavored Honey

Heady with the essence of sweet summer berries, this honey is sublime when served with breads, scones, or muffins. Prepare it in the warm months when the berries are in season, to savor in the cold of winter.

Makes 2 ½ cups

2 cups (16 ounces) light-colored honey
½ cup fresh raspberries or strawberries

In a small saucepan, stir the honey over medium heat until warmed through. Add the berries and stir gently. Pour the honey into a heatproof jar and cool to room temperature. Cover tightly and let the honey stand at room temperature for 3 days, then refrigerate.

Berry-Flavored Honey and Orange Honey

Compound Herb Butter

Compound butters are well-spiced spreads generally made several days before serving so the flavors have time to mingle. Try one on thinly sliced white bread or an herb-flavored bread. It is also delicious on a delicate tea sandwich made with ham, turkey, or chicken.

Makes 1 cup

¼ cup lightly packed fresh basil, parsley, or cilantro leaves

1 medium scallion, white part only, chopped

½ cup (1 stick) cold butter, cut into pieces

1 teaspoon freshly squeezed lemon juice

¼ teaspoon dry mustard

¼ teaspoon freshly ground white pepper

¼ teaspoon salt

Few drops of bottled hot pepper sauce

1. In a food processor, combine the herbs and scallion. Pulse until both are finely chopped. Add the rest of the ingredients and process until the mixture is fluffy, scraping the sides often.

2. Scrape the butter onto a work surface and, with dry, cool hands, fashion it into a roll. Wrap the roll in plastic wrap and refrigerate for up to 1 week. For longer storage, wrap aluminum foil around the plastic and freeze the butter for a month or so.

3. Let the refrigerated butter stand at room temperature for 15 to 20 minutes before using and, if frozen, for 2 hours.

Sage Cheese Butter

Sage is a strong-flavored herb, so do resist the temptation to add more than recommended. This butter is wonderful on a rustic, just-baked peasant loaf. Here, we mix it with Parmesan and a little chopped parsley.

Makes 1 cup

½ cup (1 stick) butter, softened

2 tablespoons grated Parmesan cheese

2 tablespoons chopped fresh sage, or 1 teaspoon dried rubbed sage

1 tablespoon chopped fresh parsley, or 1 teaspoon dried parsley flakes

1. In a small bowl, beat the ingredients with an electric mixer set at medium speed until they are light and fluffy.

2. Cover the bowl and let the butter stand for 3 to 3½ hours to give the flavors time to blend.

3. Refrigerate, well-covered, for up to 3 days if you have used fresh herbs, and for 1 week or so if you have used dried herbs.

Tarragon-Mustard Butter

The mustard seed lends a zesty flavor to this butter. It's particularly good with thin slices of baked ham and a few sprigs of watercress tucked between slices of whole-wheat or white bread.

Makes ½ cup

½ cup (1 stick) butter, softened

2 tablespoons chopped fresh tarragon, or 2 teaspoons dried tarragon leaves

½ teaspoon mustard seed, crushed

1. In a small bowl, beat all the ingredients with an electric mixer set at medium speed until they are light and fluffy.

2. Cover the bowl and let the butter stand at room temperature for 3 to 3½ hours to give the flavors time to blend.

3. Refrigerate the butter well-covered for up to 3 days if you have used fresh tarragon, and for 1 week or so if you have used dried tarragon.

Blackberry Syrup

As with Spiced Blackberry Jam, fresh blackberries are best here, but cultivated boysenberries or frozen berries also work well. Prepared with raspberries, the syrup is so deeply red it reminds one of liquid garnets.

Makes 2 cups of syrup with pulp, or 1 cup strained

3 cups fresh blackberries

¾ cup sugar

1¼ teaspoons grated lemon zest

⅓ water

1. In a heavy 3-quart saucepan, combine all the ingredients and mix gently. Cook over medium heat, stirring constantly, until the sugar dissolves.

2. Bring the syrup to a boil over medium-high heat. Reduce the heat and simmer, uncovered, for about 8 minutes, stirring occasionally, until the fruit is soft.

3. Cook for another 2 to 3 minutes and gently mash the berries against the side of the pan with the back of a wooden spoon.

4. Cool the syrup to lukewarm. If desired, strain the fruit from the syrup by pressing the syrup through a sieve. Pour into a jar. Cover and refrigerate for up to 2 weeks.

Start your morning with Spiced Blackberry Jam on toast, or Blackberry Syrup on waffles, if you prefer.

Spiced Blackberry Jam

If you can, make this piquant jam with the wild, fresh blackberries that grow along country roads. If you have no access to wild berries, choose the boysenberries or blackberries available at farmers' markets. However, a craving for this sweet, cinnamon-touched jam should not go unanswered: It is delicious made with frozen berries, too.

Makes 1 quart

1 quart fresh blackberries,
or frozen loose-pack unsweetened blackberries, thawed

¼ cup freshly squeezed lemon juice

4½ cups sugar

1½ teaspoons finely grated lemon zest

¼ teaspoon ground cinnamon

Cinnamon sticks

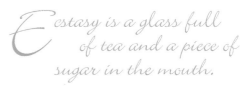

Ecstasy is a glass full of tea and a piece of sugar in the mouth.

—Alexander Pushkin

1. In a heavy 4-quart saucepan, combine the berries and lemon juice. Bring to a boil over medium-high heat, stirring often.

2. Stir in the sugar, lemon zest, and ground cinnamon, and let the mixure boil to dissolve the sugar.

3. Reduce the heat to medium and boil gently for about 15 minutes, stirring often, until the temperature reaches 220°F on a candy thermometer. (Subtract 2°F for each 1,000 feet above sea level.)

4. Remove the pot from the heat. Stir the jam with a long-handled spoon and skim off any foam that rises to the top.

5. Ladle the jam into hot, sterilized half-pint canning jars, leaving a ¼-inch space on top. Place a piece of cinnamon stick in the jam in each jar. Seal with canning lids according to manufacturer's instructions.

6. Cool the jars upright on a wire rack. Store in the refrigerator up to 1 month. For longer storage, process the jars in a boiling-water bath for 5 minutes after sealing. (Add an additional minute of processing time for each 1,000 feet above sea level.) Cool on a rack and label. Store the jars in a cool, dry, and dark place.

Opposite: Tea and toast, the perfect combination made even better with jam.

Cookies

Throughout this section, you'll find recipes for a charming assortment of cookies, from madeleines and meringues to gingerbread and sugar cookies. For additional options, see the following recipes within the party menus:

Heart Cookies, page 104

Jam Cookies, page 70

Above and opposite: For those of you who never have a cup of tea without a cookie to dip in it, we've provided a range of recipes to keep your cookie jar full.

Raspberry and Lemon Curd Hearts

These little heart-shaped sandwiches, with dark red raspberry jam or bright lemon curd peeking through them, are festive on the tea table. If you use cookie cutters that measure differently from the ones we call for, be sure the bread is large enough to accommodate them.

Makes 12 heart sandwiches

24 slices firm, thin white bread, each 3 inches wide

¼ cup raspberry jam

¼ cup lemon curd

1. Cut a heart shape from each of the 24 slices of bread using a 2⅝-inch heart-shaped cookie cutter. In 12 of the heart-shaped pieces, use a 2-inch or smaller heart-shaped cookie cutter inside to make heart cutouts in the center of each. Discard the small heart pieces.

2. Spread 6 whole hearts with about 2 teaspoons of raspberry jam each. Spread the remaining 6 whole hearts with about 2 teaspoons of lemon curd each. Top each with a cutout heart.

3. Carefully place the sandwiches on the rack of a toaster oven and toast as you would ordinarily, until the bread is a light, golden brown. Serve immediately.

Note: If you do not have a toaster oven, toast the bread hearts for 10 to 20 seconds under a preheated broiler before spreading with jam. Turn them and toast the other sides for a few seconds, or until they are a light golden brown. Spread the whole hearts with jam or curd, as described above, and assemble. Serve immediately.

Grilled Marmalade Fingers

The essence of an authentic tea party, marmalade fingers are easy to prepare and tasty. The queen in the nursery rhyme may have preferred butter to marmalade for her bread, but with these dainty fingers you can enjoy both.

Makes 18 fingers

6 slices whole-wheat bread

5 to 6 tablespoons butter, softened

4 to 6 tablespoons orange marmalade

¼ cup coarsely chopped pecans

1. Preheat the broiler. Toast the bread slices lightly.

2. Spread each slice sparingly with butter, then spread each with 2 to 3 teaspoons of marmalade, being sure the marmalade goes all the way to the edges. Sprinkle the chopped pecans evenly over the marmalade-covered bread slices.

3. Arrange the toasts on a baking sheet, marmalade side up, and place them under the broiler for 1 to 2 minutes, or until the marmalade begins to bubble and pecans are lightly charred.

4. Carefully cut off the charred crusts and then cut each slice into 3 strips, or "fingers." Handle the toast carefully as the marmalade will be very hot. Serve the marmalade fingers immediately.

Meringue Kisses

Just airy swirls of sweet flavor, Meringue Kisses are so easy to make. But it is not a good idea to make meringues on a humid day, as they will never harden to the right consistency: crispy outside, a little chewy within.

Makes 5 dozen kisses

4 egg whites, at room temperature

⅛ teaspoon cream of tartar

1 cup sugar

1. Preheat the oven to 225°F and butter 2 baking sheets. Line each baking sheet with parchment or wax paper, and butter well.

2. In the small bowl of an electric mixer, beat the egg whites at high speed until they are frothy. Add the cream of tartar. Continue beating at high speed and add the sugar, 1 tablespoon at a time, beating for 30 seconds after each addition for the first ½ cup. For the second ½ cup, beat the meringue for 10 to 15 seconds after each tablespoon of sugar. Total beating time will be about 10 minutes, at which point the meringue should be stiff, smooth, and glossy.

3. Spoon the meringue into a large pastry bag fitted with a large star tip. Pipe swirled, peaked "kiss" shapes onto the baking sheets, leaving about 1 inch between each.

4. Bake the meringues for 60 minutes, or until they are slightly golden. Turn the oven off, but do not open the door. Let the kisses stand in the turned-off oven for 1 hour. Serve right away, or store in an airtight container.

A Sweets Tea

Ambrosia Torte
White Grape Tart
Rose Water Sugar Cookies
Meringue Kisses
Feathery Chocolate Pudding
Country French Prune Pudding
Old-Fashioned Sauces for Puddings
Ginger Pear Delight
Rosy Yogurt Cooler

Meringue Kisses and Jam Cookies

Lime Wafers

Crisp, thin, and light, these sprightly lime-flavored wafers are spiced with just a wisp of ginger. For nice thin wafers, roll in only one direction, beginning at the middle and working outward.

Makes about 4 dozen wafers

1 cup (2 sticks) butter, softened

2 cups sugar

3 eggs

1 teaspoon grated lime zest

3 tablespoons freshly squeezed lime juice

½ teaspoon salt

¼ teaspoon ground ginger

5 cups all-purpose flour, sifted

1. In the large bowl of an electric mixer, cream the butter for 2 to 3 minutes at medium speed until it is light. Gradually add the sugar, beating for 2 to 3 minutes, until the mixture is light and fluffy. Scrape the sides of the bowl often. Add the eggs, lime zest, lime juice, salt, and ginger. Beat well. With the mixer at low speed, gradually beat in the flour until well blended.

2. Divide the dough into 4 equal pieces. Wrap each piece in plastic wrap and refrigerate for at least 2 hours.

3. Preheat the oven to 375°F. Butter 2 baking sheets.

4. On a well-floured work surface, roll 1 piece of chilled dough into an 8½-inch-diameter circle about ¼ inch thick. Keep the remaining dough refrigerated until you are ready to roll it.

5. When a piece of the dough is rolled out, cut out the wafers with a 2-inch round cookie cutter or an upturned glass. Using a floured metal spatula, lift the cookies and arrange them 1 inch apart on the baking sheets. Repeat with the remaining dough.

6. Bake the cookies for 15 to 17 minutes, or until the edges of the wafers are lightly browned. Cool the wafers on wire racks. Serve the cookies or store them in an airtight container.

Lime Wafers

158

Rose Water Sugar Cookies

These big, crisp sugar cookies are sweet and subtly scented with rose water.

Makes 5 dozen cookies

4½ cups all-purpose flour, sifted

1 teaspoon baking powder

1 teaspoon baking soda

1 teaspoon salt

1 cup (2 sticks) butter, softened

1½ cups sugar

2 eggs

1 cup sour cream

1 tablespoon rose water

Sugar

1. In a medium bowl, sift together the flour, baking powder, baking soda, and salt.

2. In the large bowl of an electric mixer, cream the butter and sugar at medium speed for 4 to 5 minutes until it is light and fluffy, scraping down the side of the bowl often. Add the eggs, one at time, beating well after each addition. With the mixer at low speed, add the dry ingredients to the egg mixture, alternating with the sour cream and rose water. Beat well.

3. Divide the dough into 3 pieces and wrap each in plastic wrap. Refrigerate for at least 4 hours or overnight.

4. Preheat the oven to 375°F. On a well-floured surface, roll each piece of the chilled dough into a circle about ¼ inch thick. Cut the cookies with floured 3-inch cookie cutters.

5. Using a floured metal spatula, arrange the cookies 1 inch apart on unbuttered baking sheets. Sprinkle the cookies with sugar and bake for 12 minutes or until they are lightly browned. Cool on racks and serve.

Madeleines

Of all the cakes, cookies, and sandwiches that are passed as tea is poured, none equals the perfection of a fragrant, tenderly warm madeleine. The cookie has a delicate crumb and a fragile flavor that gently echoes a few drops of fresh lemon juice.

Makes 2 dozen cookies

⅔ cup confectioners' sugar

3 eggs

1 egg yolk

Juice of ½ lemon

Pinch of salt

1¼ cups all-purpose flour, sifted

½ cup (1 stick) butter, melted

1. Preheat the oven to 350°F and butter 24 madeleine molds.

2. In the medium bowl of an electric mixer, beat the sugar, whole eggs, egg yolk, lemon juice, and salt at low speed until they are well blended. Fold in the flour until it is well combined. Slowly add the melted butter to the mixture, and stir to blend.

3. Spoon the batter into the molds, filling them no more than ⅔ full.

4. Bake the cookies for 20 to 25 minutes, or until they are slightly golden. Unmold and cool the cookies on wire racks and serve.

Dreamy Almond Cookies

Light and crisp and buttery, Dreamy Almond Cookies are ever so easy to eat. The batter is simple to mix, but since it must chill for at least an hour, makes these cookies when you have time to plan ahead.

Makes 4 dozen cookies

2 cups all-purpose flour

1 teaspoon baking powder

1 cup (2 sticks) butter, softened

¾ cup sugar

2 teaspoons vanilla extract

24 blanched whole almonds, halved lengthwise

1. In a medium bowl, sift together the flour and baking powder. Set aside.

2. In the medium bowl of an electric mixer, beat the butter, sugar, and vanilla at medium speed until the mixture is light and fluffy, scraping the sides of the bowl often. Add the dry ingredients to the creamed mixture until it is blended and smooth. Cover the dough with plastic wrap and refrigerate for 1 hour.

3. Preheat the oven to 300°F. Roll the chilled dough into 1-inch balls. Place them 2½ inches apart on unbuttered baking sheets. Gently press an almond half in the top of each ball.

4. Bake the cookies for 25 minutes, or until they turn a very pale golden color. The cookies will be very light and crisp. Cool them on wire racks. Serve the cookies or store them in an airtight container.

Black Walnut Linzer Hearts

These little jam-filled black walnut cookies are the jewels of the tea table. However, since black walnuts are a little tricky to find, you may prefer to use English walnuts.

Makes 1 dozen cookies

1 cup (2 sticks) butter

½ cup granulated sugar

2 cups all-purpose flour

⅓ cup ground black or English walnuts

½ teaspoon salt

1 to 2 tablespoons raspberry or blackberry jam

Confectioners' sugar

1. In the medium bowl of an electric mixer, cream the butter and granulated sugar at high speed until light and fluffy. Add the flour, walnuts, and salt. Stir until the mixture forms a soft dough; wrap in plastic wrap and refrigerate for 45 minutes.

2. Preheat the oven to 375°F. Butter 2 baking sheets.

3. On a floured work surface, roll the chilled dough into a circle about ¼ inch thick. Cut out heart shapes using a 2⅝-inch heart-shaped cookie cutter. Using a 2-inch or smaller heart-shaped cookie cutter, cut out the centers of the hearts. Carefully place the cookies on the baking sheets about 1 inch apart.

4. Bake for 12 to 14 minutes, or until the cookies are lightly browned. Cool the cookies on wire racks.

5. Spread each whole heart cookie with ½ to 1 teaspoon of jam, leaving a border around

the edge. Sift confectioners' sugar on the cookies with the cut-out hearts. Place these, sugar side up, on the jam-topped cookies. Serve the cookies immediately or store in an airtight container.

Gingerbread Girls and Boys

Big and chewy, these gingerbread cookies are loved by children, as well as the child in all of us. Make them for a child's party or during the holiday season for a fun and nostalgic treat. Besides the familiar gingerbread man cutter, girl and boy versions can be found at specialty bake stores. When you are decorating the cookies, you may want to cut the raisins in two to make more convincing eyes and buttons.

Makes 3 dozen cookies

5 cups all-purpose flour

1½ teaspoons baking soda

1 tablespoon ground ginger

2 teaspoons dried ground lemon zest

1 teaspoon ground cinnamon

½ teaspoon ground cloves

⅓ teaspoon nutmeg

1 cup (2 sticks) butter, softened

1 cup sugar

1 egg

1 cup molasses

2 tablespoons freshly squeezed lemon juice

Raisins, for decoration

1. In a medium bowl, stir together the flour, baking soda, ginger, lemon zest, cinnamon, cloves, and nutmeg. Set aside.

2. In the medium bowl of an electric mixer, cream the butter and sugar at medium speed for about 5 minutes, until the mixture is fluffy, scraping the sides of the bowl often. Add the egg, molasses, and lemon juice to the mixture. Beat until blended. Gradually add the dry ingredients into the egg mixture with the mixer set at low speed until blended.

3. Divide the dough into 4 equal pieces. Wrap each piece in plastic wrap and refrigerate for at least 3 hours.

4. Preheat the oven to 375°F. Butter 2 baking sheets and line them with parchment or wax paper. Lightly butter the paper.

5. On a well-floured work surface, roll 1 piece of chilled dough into a circle about ⅛ inch thick. Keep the remaining dough refrigerated until you are ready to roll it.

6. When a piece of the dough is rolled, flour a 4-inch gingerbread cookie cutter and cut out as many cookies as possible from it. Gather together the scraps, reroll them, and cut out more cookies. Using a floured metal spatula, gently lift the cookies and put them 1 inch apart on the baking sheets. Decorate with raisin buttons down their fronts and with raisins for eyes. Repeat with the remaining pieces of dough.

7. Bake the cookies for 6 to 7 minutes, or until they are puffed and set.

8. Cool the cookies on the baking sheets for 1 minute and then transfer them to wire racks to cool completely. Serve the cookies or store in an airtight container.

A nother novelty is the tea-party, an extraordinary meal in that, being offered to persons that have already dined well, it supposes neither appetite nor thirst, and has no object but distraction, no basis but delicate enjoyment.

—Bernard-Paul Heroux

Cakes, Tarts, and Puddings

Throughout this section, you'll find recipes for a delightful assortment of cakes, tarts, and puddings that will make any occasion special. For additional options, see the following recipes within the party menus:

Butter Sponge Cake, page 95

Lemon Cupcakes, page 87

Orange-Marmalade Cake, page 78

Poppy Seed–Jam Tarts, page 64

Above and opposite: Take the time to bake one of our teacakes or tarts. Trust us, your efforts will be richly rewarded.

Lemon-Ginger Pound Cake

Lemon and fresh ginger are a perfect marriage, and nowhere is their compatibility more apparent than in this buttery pound cake glazed with sweetened lemon juice.

🍃 *Makes 16 servings*

3 cups all-purpose flour

2 teaspoons baking powder

½ teaspoon salt

1 cup (2 sticks) butter, softened

2 cups sugar

4 eggs

1 cup milk

Grated zest of 2 lemons

2 teaspoons grated fresh ginger

¼ cup sugar, for glaze

3 tablespoons freshly squeezed lemon juice, for glaze

1. Preheat the oven to 350°F. Butter and flour four 7½- by 3½-inch loaf pans, or two 9- by 5- by 3-inch loaf pans. Shake out any excess flour.

2. In a medium bowl, sift together the flour, baking powder, and salt. Set aside.

3. In the large bowl of an electric mixer, cream the butter and sugar at medium speed until they are fluffy, scraping the sides of the bowl often. Add the eggs one at a time, beating well after each addition. Add the flour mixture to the batter, alternating it with the milk and beating at low speed until blended. Fold in the lemon zest and ginger. Divide the batter evenly among the prepared pans.

4. Bake for 45 to 50 minutes for four small loaves, or 60 to 65 minutes for two large loaves, until a toothpick inserted into the center of a cake comes out clean.

5. Cool the cakes still in the pans for 10 minutes on wire racks. While the cakes are cooling in the pans, combine the sugar and lemon juice in a small bowl and mix well.

6. Remove the cakes from the pans and set them on racks placed over sheet pans or foil. Brush the lemon glaze on the cakes while they are still hot.

Blackberry Jam Cake

The familiar flavor of lemonade lightly permeates this simple cream-frosted cake. Inside, deep, dark, sweet blackberry jam provides a delightful contrast of taste, texture, and color. Festoon your cake with the season's first pansies for true high summer tea.

🍃 *Makes 12 servings*

2¼ cups cake flour

1¼ cups granulated sugar

2 teaspoons baking powder

¼ teaspoon salt

¼ cup frozen lemonade concentrate, thawed

1¼ cups heavy cream, chilled

3 eggs

½ teaspoon vanilla extract

Frosting

1½ cups heavy cream, chilled

2 tablespoons confectioner's sugar

2 tablespoons frozen lemonade
concentrate, thawed

Filling and garnish

¾ cup blackberry jam or preserves

Purple pansies and fresh blackberries
(optional)

TO MAKE THE CAKE

1. Preheat the oven to 350°F. Butter and flour two 8-inch round cake pans. Shake out any excess flour.

2. In a small bowl, stir together the flour, sugar, baking powder, and salt. Set aside.

3. In a chilled small mixing bowl of an electric mixer, gradually beat the lemonade concentrate into the cream at low speed. Increase the speed to medium and beat until the mixture holds it shape. Transfer the mixture to a large bowl and set aside.

4. In another small bowl of an electric mixer, beat the eggs and vanilla with clean beaters at high speed until the mixture is thick and lemon colored, about 5 minutes. Fold the egg mixture into the cream mixture. Then gently fold in the dry ingredients. When evenly mixed, divide the batter equally between the prepared pans.

5. Bake the cake for 30 to 35 minutes, or until a toothpick inserted in the center comes out clean.

6. Cool the cakes in the pans on wire racks for 10 minutes; then remove the layers and let them cool completely on the racks.

TO MAKE THE FROSTING

In a chilled bowl of an electric mixer, combine the cream and confectioners' sugar. With the mixer set at low speed, gradually beat in the lemonade concentrate. Increase the speed to medium and beat until stiff peaks form.

TO ASSEMBLE THE CAKE

Arrange one cake layer on a serving plate and spread it with jam or preserves. Place the other layer on top. Cover the top and sides of the cake with the frosting and refrigerate for at least 2 hours. Decorate with pansies and blackberries, if you desire.

Blackberry Jam Cake

Hickory Nut Butter Cakes

The glaze for these little treasures is similar to the one for the Ambrosia Torte (page 175), but the cake, chock-full of buttery hickory nuts, tastes quite unique. The fluted cakes look elegant set on a large doily-lined pedestal cake stand or mixed with an assortment of cookies and slices of dessert bread.

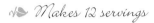 *Makes 12 servings*

3 cups all-purpose flour

2 teaspoons baking powder

1 cup (2 sticks) butter, softened

2 cups granulated sugar

Grated zest from 1 orange

3 eggs

1 cup milk

1 teaspoon vanilla extract

1 cup chopped hickory nuts, pecans, or walnuts

Orange Glaze

1 cup confectioners' sugar

¼ teaspoon vanilla extract

4 to 6 teaspoons orange juice

TO MAKE THE CAKES

1. Preheat the oven to 350°F. Spray twelve 1-cup fluted mini-tube pan cups with non-stick cooking spray.

2. In a medium bowl, combine the flour and baking powder. Stir a few times to mix well. Set aside.

3. In the large bowl of an electric mixer, cream the butter and sugar at medium speed for about 5 minutes, or until they are light and fluffy, scraping the sides of the bowl often.

Hickory Nut Butter Cake

Add the orange zest and the eggs, one at a time, beating well after each addition. Add the dry ingredients to the egg mixture, alternating it with the milk. With the mixer at low speed, blend the ingredients after each addition. When all the flour and milk are incorporated into the batter, add the vanilla and mix well. Fold in the nuts. Spread the batter evenly in the prepared cups, using about ⅔ cup of batter for each.

4. Bake for 20 to 25 minutes, or until a toothpick inserted in the center of a cake comes out clean.

5. Set the pans on wire racks and let the cakes cool for 15 minutes. Run a knife carefully around the edges of the cakes to loosen them. Remove the cakes from the pans and cool completely on the racks.

TO MAKE THE GLAZE

In a small bowl, combine the confectioners' sugar, vanilla, and enough orange juice to achieve a thin consistency. Drizzle the glaze over the cooled cakes.

166

Chocolate-Walnut Torte

Use your favorite pie crust recipe or the pastry from the Honey Tart (page 168) for this sumptuous chocolate and nut extravaganza.

When caramelizing the sugar for the filling, be sure to use a heavy saucepan. If the pan is too thin, the sugar will burn. Stir the sugar 3 or 4 times a minute at the beginning of the cooking; once the sugar begins to stick together and form tiny clumps, it is crucial to stir it constantly.

Be sure to take the pan from the heat before stirring in the cream. If you do not, the hot sugar may seize when the cream is added and form a hard mass in the bottom of the pan, which is virtually impossible to dissolve. When heating cream and sugar, make sure the heat is turned down to medium-low; the moderate heat will prevent seizing while the last of the sugar crystals dissolves. Let the mixture cool off the heat.

Makes 6 to 8 servings

Caramel-Walnut Filling

1 cup sugar

1 cup heavy cream, warmed

1/4 cup light rum

3 tablespoons honey

About 2 2/3 cups walnuts, chopped

Torte

Pastry for a 2-crust, 9-inch pie

2 ounces semisweet chocolate, chopped

1 egg

1 tablespoon water

TO MAKE THE FILLING

1. In a heavy medium-size saucepan, heat the sugar over medium-low heat, stirring often, until the sugar starts to form small clumps. Continue to cook, stirring constantly, until the sugar turns golden but has not melted. This will take about 20 to 25 minutes. Remove the pan from the heat.

2. Slowly stir in the warmed cream. The sugar will become lumpy. Return the pan to medium-low heat for about 5 minutes, and stir slowly to dissolve most of the sugar lumps. Remove the pan from the heat. Add the rum and honey and mix well. Stir in the walnuts.

TO ASSEMBLE THE TORTE

1. Preheat the oven to 350°F. Butter a 9-inch tart pan with a removable bottom.

2. On a lightly floured surface, roll out two thirds of the pastry into a 9-inch circle. Line the prepared tart pan with the pastry, pressing it into the bottom and sides of the pan. Set the tart pan on a baking sheet and sprinkle the chopped chocolate over the bottom of the pastry shell. Pour the caramel-nut filling over the chocolate.

3. Roll out the remaining pastry on a lightly floured work surface. Cut the pastry into 1/2-inch strips. Weave the strips diagonally to form a lattice top on the torte. Crimp the edges of the torte.

4. In a small bowl, beat together the egg and water with a fork. Brush the pastry with the egg wash.

5. Bake for 50 minutes, or until the filling is bubbling and the crust is golden brown. Cool the torte in the pan on a wire rack.

Honey Tart

Tender crust and pretty latticework make this rich tart, baked with a honey-kissed cheese filling, especially appealing. When weaving a lattice top, be sure the work surface is well floured to prevent the strips from sticking and tearing when you lift them up to arrange on the tart. Lay them gently on the filling, doing so at an angle from your vantage point. This will help you keep the strips looking even and straight. And finally, avoid temptations to press the strips into the filling or edges of the pastry to ensure that the lattice will bake without cracking.

Makes 8 servings

Cheese Filling

1½ cups (12 ounces) cream cheese, softened

¾ cup (6 ounces) cottage cheese

⅓ cup honey, preferably orange blossom

3 tablespoons sour cream

3 tablespoons honey liqueur or orange liqueur

2 teaspoons grated orange zest

Pastry

2 cups all-purpose flour

¼ cup sugar

Pinch of salt

10 tablespoons (1¼ sticks) butter, cut into pieces

1 tablespoon grated orange zest

2 egg yolks, beaten

2 tablespoons cold water

TO MAKE THE CHEESE FILLING

In the small bowl of an electric mixer beat the cream cheese, cottage cheese, honey, sour cream, liqueur, and orange zest at medium speed until blended. Cover and refrigerate for 2 to 3 hours.

TO MAKE THE PASTRY

1. In the bowl of a food processor fitted with a metal blade, combine the flour, sugar, and salt. Distribute the butter and orange zest over the flour mixture. Process with on-off pulses until the mixture resembles fine meal.

2. In a small mixing bowl, whisk together the egg yolks and cold water. With the processor running, gradually add the yolks to the other ingredients just until blended and cohesive. Do not mix so much that the dough forms a ball.

3. Turn the dough out onto a lightly floured work surface and knead it with your fingertips until it forms a ball. Wrap the dough in plastic wrap and refrigerate it for at least 30 minutes.

4. Take the chilled dough from the refrigerator and divide it into 2 pieces, one containing about two-thirds of the dough, the other about a third. Rewrap the smaller piece and refrigerate it. Roll out the larger piece of dough on a floured surface into a 12-inch square. Line a 10-inch square tart pan with the dough, pressing it into the bottom and the sides. Trim the edges of the dough with a sharp knife. Place the tart pan on a baking sheet and freeze for 1 hour.

🎵 Honey Tart

TO ASSEMBLE THE TART

1. If you turned off the oven after making the pastry, preheat it to 350°F. Fill the cooled pastry with the cheese filling.

2. On a floured work surface, roll the remaining piece of pastry into a 10-inch square. Cut into 1/2-inch-wide strips. Arrange half the strips in rows on top of the tart. Lay the remaining strips at an angle over the first strips. Trim the ends of the pastry strips so that they are flush with the edge of the tart. Do not attach the pastry strips to the baked crust.

3. Bake the assembled tart set on a baking sheet for 40 to 45 minutes, or until the filling is set. Cool the tart on a wire rack.

5. Preheat the oven to 350°F. Prick the cold pastry all over with a fork. Line the pastry with a double thickness of foil and fill the foil with dried beans, rice, or pastry weights to keep the pastry flat during baking.

6 Bake for 15 minutes, or until the pastry begins to brown around the edges. Remove the foil and weights. Prick the pastry again and continue baking for 5 to 10 minutes, or until it is golden.

7. Cool the baked tart shell on a wire rack. Do not turn off the oven unless you do not plan to assemble and bake the tart for several hours.

Meanwhile, have a cup of tea. The afternoon glow is brightening the bamboos, the fountains are bubbling with delight, the soughing of the pines is heard in our kettle. Let us dream of evanescence, and linger in the beautiful foolishness of things.

—Kazuko Okakura, *The Book of Tea*

Lily of the Valley Cake

When selecting a filling for this traditional butter cake, choose one that complements the flavoring in the buttercream. For instance, if you decide to flavor the buttercream with Framboise, spread strawberry or raspberry preserves between the cake layers. If you choose to omit the liqueur and use only lemon zest, you may decide to fill the cake with lemon curd.

Makes 10 to 12 servings

6 eggs, at room temperature

1 cup sugar

2 teaspoons finely grated lemon zest

1½ cups all-purpose flour

¼ cup (½ stick) butter, melted

French Buttercream

1⅔ cups sugar

½ cup water

6 egg whites, at room temperature

¼ teaspoon cream of tartar

Pinch of salt

2½ cups (5 sticks) butter, softened

2 teaspoons finely grated lemon zest

2 teaspoons liqueur such as Grand Marnier, Kahlúa, Framboise, or your favorite, optional

Filling

About ½ cup fruit preserves or jam or lemon curd

TO MAKE THE CAKE

1. Preheat the oven to 350°F. Butter and flour two 8-inch round cake pans. Line the bottom of each pan with wax paper. Butter and flour the wax paper and the sides of the pans. Shake out any excess flour.

2. In a medium saucepan, whisk the eggs with the sugar and lemon zest until they are blended. Set the pan over low heat and whisk until the mixture is warm.

3. Pour the mixture into a large bowl of an electric mixer and beat at high speed for about 7 minutes, or until the batter is light and fluffy.

4. Slowly sift the flour over the batter and gently fold it in. Do not overmix. Gradually fold in the melted butter, folding just until the batter is smooth. Fill the prepared pans with equal amounts of batter. Tap them gently on the counter to release air bubbles.

5. Bake the cakes with the pans set on a baking sheet for 28 to 30 minutes, or until the cake is golden and springs back when gently touched in the center.

6. Cool the cakes still in the pans on wire racks for 5 minutes. Invert the cakes onto the racks and peel off the paper. Allow them to cool thoroughly.

TO MAKE THE BUTTERCREAM

1. Combine the sugar and water in a large, heavy saucepan. Slowly stir to dissolve some of the sugar.

2. Cook the mixture over high heat, without stirring, until it is boiling. Cover the pan, reduce the heat to medium-high, and boil for 5 minutes.

3. Remove the lid and let the syrup boil until it reaches 242°F on a candy thermometer.

4. Meanwhile, in the medium bowl of an electric mixer, beat the egg whites, cream of tartar, and salt at high speed until stiff peaks form.

5. As soon as the syrup reaches the desired temperature, add it in droplets to the beaten egg whites, continuing to beat them at high speed. When a third of the syrup is incorporated, add the rest in a slow steady stream while still beating at high speed. Beat the meringue until it cools, about 10 to 12 minutes.

6. While beating the meringue, cream the softened butter in a medium bowl, using another electric mixer or hand-held mixer, until it is light and fluffy. If you have only one mixer, cream the butter before you begin making the meringue and hold it at room temperature.

7. Once the meringue is cool, beat in the butter, a dessert-spoonful at a time. (If the meringue is not cool, the butter will melt.) Add the lemon zest and the liqueur. Beat briefly to incorporate.

A Garden Tea

Spinach Cheese Tartlets
Blackberry Muffin Miniatures
Spiced Blackberry Jam
Lily of the Valley Cake
Country Peach and Plum Tart
Marmalade Torte Paradiso
Orange-Clove Tea
Iced Lemon-Mint Tea

TO ASSEMBLE THE CAKE

1. Brush the crumbs off the cake and, if necessary, even the layers with a knife.

2. Place the bottom layer on a serving plate. Spread it with fruit preserves, jam, or lemon curd.

3. Position the second layer on the filling. Frost the sides and top of the cake with a thin layer of buttercream. Refrigerate the cake for 10 to 15 minutes or until the buttercream is chilled. Frost the cake with a second, more luxurious coat of buttercream.

4. Serve the cake at once or refrigerate it for later serving. Because of the amount of butter in the frosting, the cake cannot sit at room temperature very long. Take it from the refrigerator about 30 minutes before serving to take off the chill.

Country Peach and Plum Tart

This free-form tart is summertime itself. The sweet, nutty layer of frangipane snuggled beneath the juicy plums and peaches adds an unexpected dimension of taste and texture, heightened by the crisp, fragile pastry. Traditionally, frangipane is made with eggs, sugar, and milk and flavored heavily with almond, or sometimes macaroons.

 *Makes 12 servings*

Pastry

2 cups all-purpose flour

2 teaspoons grated orange zest

1 teaspoon granulated sugar

½ teaspoon salt

½ teaspoon ground cloves

½ cup (1 stick) butter, cut into pieces

1 egg yolk

⅓ cup cold water

Frangipane

1 cup blanched slivered almonds

2 egg whites

⅔ cup confectioners' sugar

½ teaspoon almond extract

Filling

1 pound small dark plums, pitted and halved (7 or 8 plums)

¾ pound peaches, pitted and cut into eighths (about 3 peaches)

2 tablespoons granulated sugar

1 teaspoon ground cinnamon

2 tablespoons (¼ stick) butter

Glaze and Garnish

1 tablespoon plum or orange liqueur

½ cup apricot jam

Fresh mint sprigs

Whipped cream

TO MAKE THE PASTRY

1. In a large bowl, combine the flour, orange zest, sugar, salt, and cloves and mix well. Add the butter. Using a pastry blender or 2 kitchen knives, cut the butter into the mixture until it resembles coarse crumbs.

2. Add the egg yolk and cold water. Mix the dough with your hands until it forms a moist ball. Wrap the pastry dough in plastic wrap and refrigerate it for at least 45 minutes, or until you are ready to use it.

TO MAKE THE FRANGIPANE

1. In a food processor with a metal blade, process the almonds until they are pulverized, about 1 minute.

2. Add the egg whites, confectioners' sugar, and almond extract. Process until well blended and set aside.

TO MAKE THE FILLING

1. In a large bowl, combine the fruit.

2. Mix the sugar and cinnamon together and add them to the fruit. Toss lightly with the fruit.

TO ASSEMBLE THE TART

1. Preheat the oven to 400°F. On a lightly floured work surface, roll the chilled dough into a 16- by 12-inch rectangle. Gently fold the dough into quarters. Lay the folded

172

dough on an unbuttered baking sheet and unfold it. Spread the frangipane over the dough, leaving a 2-inch border on all sides. Arrange the fruit on top of the frangipane. Fold the dough's 2-inch border over the fruit to make an edge that will hold in the juices. Repair any cracks in the edge of the dough and pinch the corners together to seal. Dot the fruit with the butter.

2. Bake for 50 to 60 minutes, or until the fruit is tender and the crust is golden.

3. Cool the tart on a wire rack. Combine the liqueur and jam in a small saucepan and heat gently, stirring constantly, until the jam melts. Drizzle the apricot glaze over the fruit, add fresh mint sprigs, and serve with whipped cream.

Country Peach and Plum Tart

White Grape Tart

This cooling and simple grape tart is refreshingly delicious on a warm summer's afternoon when the tea of choice is iced and the primary pastime is pleasant conversation with dear ones. We suggest making this tart on the day you plan to serve it, as it is quite fragile.

Makes 10 servings

Zinfandel Sauce

⅓ cup all-purpose flour

½ cup granulated sugar

Pinch of salt

3 egg yolks

1 cup light cream or milk

¼ cup white zinfandel

2 to 3 drops freshly squeezed lemon juice, optional

Pastry

1¼ cups all-purpose flour

¾ cup (1½ sticks) butter, chilled and cut into pieces

¼ cup superfine sugar

Pinch of salt

1 egg, lightly beaten

Filling and Garnish

3 pounds seedless green grapes (about 7 cups stemmed grapes)

1 egg white

Superfine sugar

Confectioners' sugar

Rose geranium leaves or mint leaves

(recipe continues)

TO MAKE THE ZINFANDEL SAUCE

1. Thoroughly mix the flour, sugar, and salt in a heavy 1-quart saucepan. Add the egg yolks and $\frac{1}{2}$ cup of the cream and whisk until smooth. Gradually whisk in the remaining cream.

2. Cook the mixture over medium heat, stirring constantly with a wooden spoon for about 20 minutes, until the sauce is very thick and glossy. To prevent lumping, it may be necessary to whisk the sauce for the last few minutes of cooking.

3. Pour the sauce into a 1-quart bowl. Lay wax paper directly on its surface and refrigerate for $1\frac{1}{2}$ hours.

4. Take the chilled sauce from the refrigerator and stir in the zinfandel and, if desired, the lemon juice. Cover and chill for at least 4 more hours.

TO MAKE THE PASTRY

1. In the bowl of a food processor, add the flour, butter, sugar, salt, and egg. Process until the dough forms a ball and pulls away from the sides of the bowl. Shape the dough into a smooth ball and wrap it in plastic. Refrigerate it for 30 minutes.

2. Turn the chilled dough out onto a floured work surface and knead it with the heel of your hand until it is well blended. Using a rolling pin, roll the dough into a 14-inch circle. Drape the dough in an 11-inch tart form with a removable bottom and set on a baking sheet. Press the dough into the tart form and trim the excess. If you prefer, the dough can be patted into the tart form. Cover and refrigerate for 45 minutes.

TO ASSEMBLE THE TART

1. Preheat the oven to 400°F. Remove the stems from the grapes and wash the grapes briefly in cold water. Dry them well on clean dishtowels or paper towels.

2. Prick the sides and bottom of the chilled tart shell with a fork and bake it for about 25 minutes, or until it is golden brown. If the pastry puffs or bubbles during baking, prick the bottom of the tart again. Remove the tart from the oven and cool it completely on a wire rack.

3. In a small bowl, beat the egg white with a fork. Place some superfine sugar in a shallow dish or pie plate. Dip 2 cups of grapes first in the egg white and then in the superfine sugar. Dry on wire racks—the grapes will look frosted.

4. Just before serving, combine 3 cups of unfrosted grapes and $\frac{2}{3}$ cup of the zinfandel sauce. Spoon the grapes evenly over the bottom of the cooled tart shell. Top with the rest of the unfrosted grapes and sprinkle the tart with confectioners' sugar.

5. Garnish the tart with frosted grapes and fresh rose geranium leaves or mint leaves. Serve the tart with the remaining zinfandel sauce.

Ambrosia Torte

This torte takes only minutes to put together and a mere half hour to bake. Beyond its simplicity, this torte is notable for its delectable flavor, highlighted by the simple glaze adorned with candied zest and almonds.

Makes 6 to 8 servings

⅔ cup all-purpose flour

½ teaspoon baking powder

⅔ cup (1⅓ sticks) butter, softened

⅔ cup granulated sugar

2 eggs

1 teaspoon almond extract, optional

Glaze and Garnish

1 tablespoon orange juice

⅓ cup confectioners' sugar

About ¾ cup chopped candied orange zest and chopped almonds

Orange sections, thinly sliced

TO MAKE THE TORTE

1. Preheat the oven to 350°F. Butter and flour an 8-inch round cake pan. Shake out any excess flour.

2. In a small bowl, sift together the flour and baking powder. Set aside.

3. In the medium bowl of an electric mixer, beat the butter and sugar at medium speed until they are creamy and fluffy, scraping the sides of the bowl often. Add the eggs and almond extract. Beat for about 2 minutes, until light and smooth. Add the dry ingredients to the creamed batter and stir thoroughly until blended. Spread the batter in the prepared pan.

4. Bake for 30 minutes, or until the top of the torte springs back when touched lightly near the center.

5. Cool the torte in the pan on a wire rack for 10 minutes. Remove the torte from the pan and allow it to cool completely on the rack. If the torte sags slightly in the center as it cools, invert it to serve.

TO MAKE THE GLAZE

Gradually stir the orange juice into the confectioners' sugar until smooth. Spread the glaze evenly over the top of the torte and sprinkle with the chopped candied orange zest, almonds, and a pinwheel of thinly sliced orange sections.

A Picnic Tea

Herbed Cream Cheese Sandwiches

Chicken-Watercress Sandwiches

Compound Herb Butter

Herb-Flavored Honey

Lime Wafers

Ambrosia Torte

Lavender and Lime Tea

Strawberry Tea

Blackberry Tarts

These little tarts are lovely to serve and their sweet cream filling and berries make them so easy to eat.

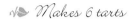 *Makes 6 tarts*

Pastry

1⅓ cups flour

1 tablespoon granulated sugar

¼ teaspoon salt

¼ cup (½ stick) butter

¼ cup lard

2 to 3 tablespoons ice water

Filling and glaze

1 8-ounce package cream cheese, softened

3 tablespoons confectioners' sugar

½ cup heavy cream

⅛ teaspoon orange extract

¼ cup red currant jelly

2 teaspoons blackberry cordial or crème de cassis

1½ cups fresh blackberries

TO MAKE THE PASTRY

1. In a medium bowl stir together the flour, granulated sugar, and salt. With a pastry blender or 2 knives, cut in the butter and lard until the pieces are pea-size.

2. Sprinkle 1 tablespoon cold water over the mixture. Toss with a fork, and push the dough to the side of the bowl. Repeat with the remaining water until all the dough is moistened. Shape the dough into a ball wrap in plastic, and refrigerate for 30 minutes.

3. Form the chilled dough into 6 equal balls. Between 2 pieces of floured wax paper, press each ball into a 5-inch circle. Press each round into a 4-inch fluted tart pan with a removable bottom and trim off any excess dough. Place the tart pans on a baking sheet and freeze about 15 minutes.

4. Preheat the oven to 400°F. Prick the cold pastry all over with a fork. Line the pastry shells with small squares of foil and fill the foil with pie weights or dried beans.

5. Bake for 10 minutes, or until the pastry begins to brown around the edges. Remove the foil and weights. Prick the pastry and bake for 7 to 9 minutes. Cool on a wire rack.

TO MAKE THE FILLING

In a small bowl of an electric mixer, combine cream cheese and confectioners' sugar at medium speed until blended. With the mixer at low speed, gradually add the heavy cream and orange extract. Beat at medium speed until mixture is thick, about 1 minute.

TO MAKE THE GLAZE

In small heavy saucepan, melt the jelly and cordial over medium heat, stirring often. Strain the mixture through cheesecloth. Let it cool slightly.

TO ASSEMBLE THE TART

Spoon the filling into the bottom of each tart shell and arrange blackberries on top of the filling. Spoon the glaze over the berries. Refrigerate the tarts until serving time.

Marmalade Torte Paradiso

Adorned with fresh orange lunettes and flourishes of whipped orange cream, this Marmalade Torte Paradiso is worthy of its name. The orange marmalade and carrots in this torte create a sweet marriage of flavors.

Makes 8 servings

4 egg yolks

½ cup plus 1 tablespoon sugar

I scant cup finely ground hazelnuts

I scant cup finely shredded carrots

2 tablespoons all-purpose flour

2 tablespoons orange marmalade

5 egg whites

Pinch of salt

Marmalade Cream Filling

1½ cups heavy cream

⅓ cup orange marmalade

Thin orange slices and whipped cream

TO MAKE THE CAKE

1. Preheat the oven to 300°F. Butter and flour two 6½- by 3-inch springform pans.

2. In a medium bowl of an electric mixer, beat the egg yolks and sugar at high speed until they are pale yellow, about 5 minutes. Add the hazelnuts, carrots, flour, and marmalade. Mix well and set aside.

3. In another medium bowl, beat the egg whites and salt at high speed until they are stiff but not dry. Gradually fold the egg whites into the batter. Pour the batter into the prepared pans.

4. Bake for 45 minutes, until the cakes are browned and just begin to pull away from the sides of the pans. Cool the cakes, still in the pans on wire racks. (The cakes will shrink and fall slightly.)

5. Loosen the edges of the cakes with a knife, and remove them from the pan. Slice each cake in two layers horizontally. (The layers are very fragile. Use a wide spatula or a flat baking sheet to move them.)

TO MAKE THE MARMALADE CREAM FILLING

In a small bowl, whip the cream until peaks form. Fold in the marmalade.

TO ASSEMBLE THE TORTE

1. Position a cake layer on a serving plate and spread ¼ of the filling on top. Add the other layers of cake with ¼ of the filling spread on each layer, including the top.

2. Garnish the torte with fresh orange slices. Pipe additional whipped cream atop the torte for decoration. Serve at once.

 Marmalade Torte Paradiso

Feathery Chocolate Pudding

For a light chocolate pudding with a soft, cake-like texture, try this at teatime. Steamed puddings have long been a tradition in the British Isles—particularly at Christmas time, when plum puddings are set on nearly every table—and as such seem an appropriate choice for tea. Our chocolate pudding, steamed a mere half hour, is light as a feather thanks to the whipped egg whites and the gentle art of steaming. Serve it with whipped cream, or with one of the Old-Fashioned Sauces for Puddings (page 180).

Makes 4 servings

1½ tablespoons butter

1 ounce semisweet chocolate

½ ounce unsweetened chocolate

2 egg whites, at room temperature

Pinch of salt

¼ cup confectioners' sugar

2 egg yolks

1 teaspoon cornstarch

½ teaspoon vanilla extract

Sweetened whipped cream

1. Set a rack in the bottom of a deep pan large enough to hold a 1-quart bowl. Butter a deep, heat proof 1-quart bowl. Add water to the pan to a depth of 2 inches. Bring the water to a boil while mixing the pudding.

2. Melt the butter in a small saucepan. In the top of a double boiler over simmering water, melt the chocolates. Cool both the butter and chocolate, and set aside.

3. In a small bowl of an electric mixer, beat the egg whites and salt at medium-high speed until they are foamy. Gradually add the confectioners' sugar, beating at high speed until soft peaks form. Set aside.

4. Put the egg yolks in another small bowl, and add, in order, the cornstarch, vanilla, melted butter, and melted chocolate. Whisk until smooth after each addition. Pour this mixture evenly over the egg whites. Fold until blended. Pour the pudding into the prepared buttered bowl and cover with foil.

5. Set the bowl on a rack in a pan of boiling water. Reduce the heat to medium. Cover the pan and steam the pudding for 30 minutes, or until it is puffed and a toothpick inserted in center comes out clean. Serve with the whipped cream.

In nothing is the English genius for domesticity more notably declared than in the institution of afternoon tea.

—George Gissing

Country French Prune Pudding

Here's another traditional pudding that's perfect for holiday teas. For prunes with a bit of an English flavor, soak them for four days in half a cup of port in a lidded pint jar. Shake the jar every so often. When it's time to make the pudding, lift the prunes from the jar with a slotted spoon and follow the recipe, omitting the kirsch.

Makes 6 servings

About 25 (8 ounces) soft, pitted prunes

Finely grated zest of 1 large orange

½ cup plus 1 tablespoons all-purpose flour

Pinch of salt

3 eggs, at room temperature

½ cup granulated sugar

1½ cups milk

4 teaspoons kirsch

Confectioners' sugar

1 cup heavy cream, for serving, optional

1. Preheat the oven to 400°F. Butter a 9½- by 1¾-inch pie plate.

2. Lay the prunes in the pie plate and sprinkle them with the orange zest.

3. In a small bowl of an electric mixer, beat the flour, salt, and 1 egg at medium speed until the flour is moistened. Add the remaining eggs, one at a time, beating well after each addition. Continue beating until the batter is very creamy, about 4 to 5 minutes. With the mixer turned down to medium-low speed, gradually add the granulated sugar, milk, and then the kirsch. Beat until the batter is smooth. Pour the batter over the prunes.

4. Bake for 45 minutes, or until the pudding is puffed and brown.

5. Dust the top of the pudding with confectioners' sugar. Serve with a pitcher of cold heavy cream to pour over the servings.

A Special Anniversary Tea

Stilton, Pear, and Watercress Savory Toasts

Sage Bread

Sage Cheese Butter

Tarragon-Mustard Butter

Blackberry Tarts

Raspberry and Lemon Curd Hearts

Black Walnut Linzer Hearts

Chocolate Walnut Torte

Lovers' Tea

White Winter Champagne Punch

Old-Fashioned Sauces for Puddings

There was a time when a pudding was not considered complete without a satiny sauce to accompany it. These three can be served with the puddings found in this book. Try the Hazelnut Sauce with the Feathery Chocolate Pudding (page 178) and the Lemon Sauce or Rose Sauce with the Country French Prune Pudding (page 179).

Makes about 1 1/2 cups

Sauce Base

1/2 cup sugar

1 tablespoon cornstarch

1 cup boiling water

1 tablespoon butter, flaked

1. In a small saucepan, combine the sugar and cornstarch. Add the boiling water and whisk until smooth.

2. Over medium-high heat, continue whisking the sugar mixture until it boils and thickens.

3. Reduce the heat to medium-low and cook for 5 minutes, whisking occasionally.

4. Add the butter, a few flakes at a time, whisking well after each addition until each flake is incorporated.

Rose Sauce

2 tablespoons red currant jelly

1/2 to 1 teaspoon rose water

Add the jelly to the hot base and whisk until melted. Whisk in the rose water. Serve the sauce warm.

Lemon Sauce

Juice and zest of 1 lemon

1/2 teaspoon ground nutmeg

Add the lemon juice, lemon zest, and nutmeg to the hot base. Whisk until melted. Serve the sauce warm.

Hazelnut Sauce

1/4 cup Frangelico liqueur

1/4 cup chopped hazelnuts

1/2 teaspoon ground cinnamon

Add the liqueur, hazelnuts, and cinnamon to the hot base. Whisk until melted. Serve the sauce warm.

Resources

Tea and Tea Equipment Defined

Tea is named in one of two ways: first, according to the region from which it originates such as Darjeeling and Ceylon; and second, because of special blending, such as Earl Grey and Marquis of Queensbury tea. Not all tea comes from the tea plant *camellia sinensis*. Nearly any drink brewed from herbs, spices, flowers, fruits, and even bark is called "tea." The most common of these teas are herb teas, also referred to as tisanes. Some flower teas, such as chamomile and elderflower, are also tisanes.

§ Above: A teapot so exotic it could be the perfect home for even the most descriminating genie.

§ Opposite: If you're a tea lover, there's a beauty to even the most utilitarian ceramic teapots.

183

TEAS

Assam: a fine-quality tea from the Assam district of India, where tea was first cultivated by the British and still remains a prized area for strong black teas.

Bancha: the everyday Japanese green tea.

Ceylon: a number of teas bear the name "Ceylon." Now known as Sri Lanka, this country produces some of the best teas in the world.

Darjeeling: a black tea from the part of India of the same name, which is in the foothills of the Himalayas. Darjeeling is considered, by some, the finest tea in the world and is the beverage of choice for many afternoon tea aficionados. Darjeeling is a classic "self drinker," which means it tastes strong and clear on its own, without blending any other tea leaves with it.

Formosa Oolong: a tea from Taiwan, which used to be Formosa, considered to be the best oolong.

Gunpowder: a high-quality green tea from China.

Keemun: an orchid-flavored tea that is considered one of the best Chinese black teas.

Lapsang Souchong: a famous black tea from China with a smoky flavor.

Nilgiri: an Indian black tea that is used almost exclusively for blending.

Oolong: a partially fermented tea that is a cross between green and black tea. Oolong tea, which is quite mild, is used for blending with black tea.

Tencha: a Japanese green tea used for tea ceremonies and considered to be the finest green tea available in Japan.

Yunnan: a fragrant and full-flavored black tea from a western province of China.

BLENDINGS

Earl Grey: a favorite blending of black teas the world around. R. Twining and Co. Ltd. originally made this tea for Charles, the second Earl Grey, but in later years other tea companies began marketing a similar blend with the same name. This is the quintessential afternoon tea.

English Breakfast Tea: a popular blending of Indian and Ceylon teas. Considered brisk enough for early morning, it is also perfectly adequate for afternoon tea.

Jasmine: a very soothing tea, made from jasmine flowers and leaves blended with green tea.

184

Orange Pekoe: a grade of tea leaf, but also a blending of good quality Ceylon tea leaves. This tea has nothing whatsoever to do with the citrus fruit.

Russian Caravan: a blend of Chinese black tea that was reportedly developed for transporting and drinking on the overland trade route between China and Russia early in the eighteenth century. Some other Chinese teas destined for Russia were first ground into powder and then compressed into bricks for easy packing. The bricks were shaved as needed for brewing with boiling water.

I am in no way interested in immortality, but only in the taste of tea.

—Lu T'ung

Tea-Brewing Tips

For complete, step-by-step instructions, see Brewing the Perfect Pot of Tea, page 122.

- Tea loves oxygen-rich water, so fill the kettle with cold water only.

- Slosh boiling water in and out of the pot to warm it. Return the kettle to a full boil and pour the water over loose tea— about one teaspoon of tea per cup, unless you like it stronger. Add up to a tablespoon per cup for more delicate green teas.

- Wide-based, round pots give the tea leaves space to unfurl.

- How long to steep tea leaves? Generally, three to five minutes, depending on your preference, but never more than five: They turn bitter. For herbal and fruit infusions, steep four to eight minutes.

- Tea bags hold leaves cut for speed; often steeping for a minute or two suffices.

FRUIT TEAS AND TISANES

Apple; Peach; Strawberry; Mango: four popular fruit teas made from the leaves and parts of the fruit.

Lemon Verbena: a tea tasting faintly of lemon and reported to reduce fever and arthritis pain.

Lemon; Orange: citrus fruits—the skins and leaves—that yield popular, refreshing teas.

Orange Blossom; Lotus; Rose; Chrysanthemum; Chamomile: a few different flower teas made from the petals and often the leaves of these flowers. All are gentle and fragrant.

Peppermint: made from crushed peppermint, or other mint leaves. This is a soothing tonic, especially for an upset stomach.

Rosehip: a bright red tea made from dried rosehips. This is a very good overall tonic for mild day-to-day ailments.

Thyme: a tea made from the dried leaves, flowers, and stems of cultivated garden thyme plants.

Tea Equipment

The Victorians, many of whom acquired great wealth during the nineteenth century, collected, among many other things, all sorts of fancy and elaborate tea implements. Silversmiths and other artisans created instruments specially designed for tasks that could just as easily been accomplished in other, if more mundane, ways.

Today, we require far fewer implements at teatime, and indeed, many of us may never own a silver tea service. Still, there exists healthy curiosity, and sometimes mild amusement about this popular teatime impedimenta.

Caddy Spoon: These spoons were used to measure tea from the caddy. Silversmiths often fashioned them to resemble shells, as the Chinese frequently used real shells to scoop loose tea.

Mote Spoon: Used to skim stray tea leaves, mote spoons are made from perforated silver and sometimes have a sharp point, which is used to clean the spout of the pot.

Muffin Dish: Since hot muffins, just toasted in the kitchen, were popular for tea, silver muffin dishes were designed with domed lids and hot water reservoirs beneath the dish to keep the muffins toasty warm.

186

Sugar Sifter; Muffineer: Shaped like a large salt or pepper shaker, these are filled with sugar or a combination of sugar and cinnamon for sprinkling on hot buttered muffins.

Sugar Tongs: Sugar tongs were more popular when sugar was served in cubes. They are most often made from silver, and may be tweezer-shaped or scissor-handled.

Tea Caddy: Caddies are containers designed to hold loose tea leaves. They were artfully fashioned from wood, porcelain, silver, or glass. Most Victorian households had at least two caddies, one for black tea, the other for green. Caddies were often kept under lock and key, to dissuade the servants from sampling the tea.

Tea Cozy: Although tea cozies were never seen at grand Victorian tea parties, they have been common in most British households since the nineteenth century. They are typically made from quilted fabric and slip over a teapot to help keep the tea warm.

Tea Strainer: These pretty strainers are designed to fit over the teacup and to catch leaves that escape from the pot when the tea is poured.

Tea Tray: Oval-shaped tea trays are made from silver or Sheffield-plate. They have a trim and a functional handle on each end for carrying. Tea trays are large enough to hold the tea service and teacups.

Tea Urn: This is a large decorative vessel for brewed tea. It is fitted with a spigot to facilitate filling smaller teapots.

Teacups: Teacups were originally shaped like coffee cups, which are less rounded. Today, a proper teacup is made from fine bone china and is slightly round with a wide, generous mouth. Early European tea and coffee cups had no handles but as afternoon tea became fashionable, handles were added to prevent ladies from burning their fingers.

Teakettle: Today, teakettles sit on stoves and are used to boil water for tea and other cooking tasks. In Victorian times, the teakettle was filled with boiling water in the kitchen and then transported to the drawing room. The kettle was set on a trivet above a spirit lamp to keep the water hot. Often, it was hinged to the trivet so that the kettle had only to be tipped for easy pouring.

Teapot: The finer teapots were made from sterling, although today many purists feel tea does not taste as good when served from a silver pot as it does from porcelain. The earliest teapots were designed similarly to straight-sided coffee and chocolate pots, but over the years they became more rounded.

Teapoy: A teapoy, a term introduced by the English who had lived in India, is a three-legged table designed to hold tea caddies and mixing containers.

Select Sources for Tea and Tea Accessories

Contact the sources listed below individually for information about hours and ordering by telephone, e-mail, fax, or mail order.

Bettys & Taylors of Harrogate

1 Parliament Street
Harrogate HGI 2QU
England
011-44-142-350-2746
www.bettysandtaylors.co.uk
Teas, confections, and Café Tea Room serving teas and meals in the traditional English style. See Web site for additional locations.

The British Shoppe and Gourmet Merchants

809 North Mills Avenue
Orlando, FL 32803
(800) 842-6674
www.thebritishshoppe.com
Traditional British teas, foods, cheeses, and tea accessories. The Front Parlour Tearoom offers lunch and afternoon tea.

Celestial Seasonings

4600 Sleepytime Drive
Boulder, CO 80301
(800) 434-4246
www.celestialseasonings.com
Tea bags for everyday from herbal to green to chai.

Crossings

(800) 209-6141
www.crossingsfrenchfood.com
French epicurean specialties, baked goods, preserves, and candies.

The Cultured Cup

13714 Gamma Road Suite 104
Dallas, TX 75244
(888) 847-8327
www.theculturedcup.com
A variety of teas, including Mariage Frères from France, tea accessories, drinking chocolate, and gourmet food products.

Dabney Herbs

P.O. Box 22061
Louisville, KY 40252
(502) 893-5198
www.dabneyherbs.com
A wide variety of organically grown herbal and green teas.

Dancing Deer Baking Company

65 Sprague Street
Boston, MA 02136
(888) 699-3337
www.dancingdeer.com
All-natural brownies, cakes, cookies, and other baked goods.

Great love affairs start with Champagne and end with tisane.

—Honoré De Balzac

Eastern Shore Tea Company
9 West Aylesbury Road
Lutherville, MD 21093
(800) 823-1408
www.baltcoffee.com
A variety of loose teas and tea bags in decorative bags and tins.

Empire Tea Services
1965 St. James Place
Columbus, IN 47203
(812) 375-1937
www.empiretea.com
Fine whole-leaf teas, tea foods, teaware, and books.

Grace Tea Company, Ltd.
14-A Craig Road
Acton, MA 01720
(978) 635-9500
www.gracetea.com
Rare teas from China, Formosa (Taiwan), India, and Ceylon (Sri Lanka) packaged in elegant black metal canisters.

Harney & Sons Fine Teas
5723 Route 22
Millerton, NY 12546
(888) 427-6398
www.harney.com
A wide variety of teas, tea accessories, tea foods, and gifts.

In Pursuit of Tea, Inc.
1435 Fourth Street
Berkeley, CA 94710
(866) TRUETEA;
www.inpursuitoftea.com
More than 30 types of teas, including white, green, black, oolong, and chai teas, from remote regions of the world. Whenever possible, sells loose-leaf, organically grown tea.

Lisa's Tea Treasures
1875 South Bascom Avenue
Suite 165
Campbell, CA 95008
(408) 371-7377
www.lisasteatreasures.com
A wide variety of teas, including black, flavored black, tisanes, and their own special tea blend, as well as tea accessories, gift sets, and a Victorian-style tearoom. See Web site for additional locations.

Mark T. Wendell Tea Company
14-A Craig Road
Acton, MA 01720
(978) 635-9200
www.marktwendell.com
A large selection of fine teas and accessories imported from around the world. Offered in both loose bulk containers and tea bags.

Mikasa
(866) 645-2721
www.mikasa.com
Fine china.

R.C. Bigelow
201 Black Rock Turnpike
Fairfield, CT 06825
(888) 244-3569
www.bigelowtea.com
Tea bags and loose-leaf tea, plus
teapots and accessories.

Republic of Tea
5 Hamilton Landing, Suite 100
Novato, CA 94949
(800) 298-4832
www.republicoftea.com
A selection of teas and tea accessories,
including caffeine-free herbal teas,
display tins, and teapots.

Royal Copenhagen
(800) 431-1992
www.royalcopenhagen.com
Fine china.

Royal Doulton
(800) 900-9973
www.royal-doulton.com
Fine china.

San Francisco Herb Company
250 14th Street
San Francisco, CA 94103
(800) 227-4530
www.sfherb.com
A variety of loose bulk teas: black,
green, white, and herbal.

Simpson & Vail
3 Quarry Road
Brookfield, CT 06804
(800) 282-8327;
(203) 775-0240
www.svtea.com
More than 150 tea varieties, as well as tea
foods and accessories.

St. John's Botanicals
P.O. Box 100
Bowie, MD 20719
(301) 262-5302
www.st-johns.com
Black, green, and herbal teas.

The Teacup
(206) 283-5931
www.seattleteacup.com
One-stop shopping for tea lovers offering tea,
accessories, tastings, and classes.

Tealuxe
0 Brattle Street
Cambridge, MA 02138
(888) TEALUXE
www.tealuxe.com
Tea bar selling more than 100 varieties
of tea by the gram, as well as gift sets
and tea accessories. Tea Academy offers
classes and tastings for tea lovers. See Web
site for additional store locations.

Todd & Holland Tea Merchants
7311 West Madison Street
Forest Park, IL 60130
(800) 747-8327
www.todd-holland.com
More than 200 varieties of loose-leaf teas,
as well as tea samplers, tea tours, and
an extensive collection of teapots,
tea accessories, and books.

Two for the Pot
200 Clinton Street
Brooklyn, NY 11201
(718) 855-8173
Loose-leaf teas and tea accessories.

Upton Tea Imports
100 Jeffrey Avenue #1
Holliston, MA 01746
(800) 234-8327
www.uptontea.com
More than 420 varieties of loose-leaf teas
plus tea accessories.

Wedgwood
(877) 900-9973
www.wedgwood.com
Fine china.

Well-Sweep Herb Farm
205 Mount Bethel Road
Port Murray, NJ 07865
(908) 852-5390
www.wellsweep.com
Herbal teas.

Wolferman's
2500 S. Pacific Highway
P.O. Box 9100
Medford, OR 97501
(800) 999-1910
www.wolfermans.com
Gourmet food gifts including English muffins, crumpets, scones, and other
baked goods.

Favorite Tea Salons
UNITED STATES & CANADA

Contact the sources listed below individually for hours, directions, and menus. Some of these tea rooms are also good sources for loose-leaf tea, tea accoutrements, and treats.

Alice's Tea Cup
102 West Seventy-Third Street
New York, NY 10023
(212) 799-3006
www.alicesteacup.com
Visit the Web site for additional Manhattan locations.

The Camellia Tea Room
828 First Street
Benicia, CA 94510
(707) 746-5293
www.camelliatearoom.com

Candlelight Inn Tearoom
30 Katharine Lee Bates Road
Falmouth, MA 01540
(508) 457-1177

Chaiwalla Tea Room
1 Main Street
Salisbury, CT 06068
(860) 435-9758

Civil-La-Tea
290 Oak Lane
Gettysburg, PA 17325
(717) 334-0992

Concord Teacakes
59 Commonwealth Avenue
Concord, MA 01742
(978) 369-7644
www.concordteacakes.com

The Dunbar House Tea Shop
1 Water Street
Sandwich, MA 02563
(508) 833-2485
www.dunbarteashop.com

Elmwood Inn Fine Teas
135 North Second Street
Danville, KY 40422
(800) 765-2139
www.elmwoodinn.com

The Empress Hotel
721 Government Street
Victoria, B.C. V8W IW5
Canada
(250) 384-8111
www.fairmont.com/empress

The Four Seasons Hotels with Tea:
www.fourseasons.com

BOSTON:
200 Boylston Street
Boston, MA 02116
(617) 338-4400

CHICAGO:
120 East Delaware Place
Chicago, IL 60611
(312) 280-8800

The Ritz-Carlton Hotel
160 East Pearson Street
Chicago, IL 60611
(312) 266-1000
www.fourseasons.com/chicagorc

LOS ANGELES:
300 South Doheny Drive
Los Angeles, CA 90048
(310) 273-2222

NEW YORK:
57 East 57th Street
New York, NY 10022
(212) 758-5700

PHILADELPHIA:
1 Logan Square
Philadelphia, PA 19103
(215) 963-1500

SEATTLE:
99 Union Street
Seattle, WA 98101
(206) 749-7000

TORONTO:
60 Yorkville Avenue
Toronto, ON M4W 0A4
Canada
(416) 964-0411

WASHINGTON, D.C.:
2800 Pennsylvania Avenue
Washington, D.C. 20007
(202) 342-0444

Four Seasons Tea Room
75 North Baldwin Avenue
Sierra Madre, CA 91024
(626) 355-0045
www.4seasonstearoom.com

Imperial Tea Court
1 Embarcadero
San Francisco, CA 94111
(510) 777-0335;
(415) 544-9830
www.imperialtea.com

The Johnston House
907 Route 228
Mars, PA 16046
(724) 625-2636
www.thejohnstonhouse.com

Lady Mendel's Tea Salon
The Inn at Irving Place
56 Irving Place
New York, NY 10003
(800) 685-1447;
(212) 533-4600
www.innatirving.com

Lady Primrose's Tea Salon
500 Crescent Court
Dallas, TX 75201
(214) 871-8334

MacNab's Tearoom
5 Yu Lu Tea Lane
Boothbay, ME 04537
(800) 884-7222;
(207) 633-7222
www.macnabstea.com

McCharles House Restaurant,
Tearoom & Gardens
335 South C Street
Tustin, CA 92780
(714) 731-4063
www.mccharleshouse.com

Murchie's Tea & Coffee
5580 Parkwood Way
Richmond, B.C. V6V 2M4
Canada
(800) 663-0400
www.murchies.com
See Web site for other locations.

The Palm Court
The Plaza Hotel
Fifth Avenue at Central Park South
New York, NY 10019
(212) 759-3000
www.fairmont.com/theplaza

Paris in a Cup
119 South Glassell Street
Orange, CA 92866
(714) 538-9411
www.parisinacup.com

Perennial Tearoom
1910 Post Alley
Seattle, WA 98101
(888) 448-4054;
(206) 448-4054
www.perennialtearoom.com

Queen Mary Tea Room
2912 Northeast 55th Street
Seattle, WA 98105
(206) 527-2770
www.queenmarytearoom.com

Royal Tea Company
5628 Main Street
Trumbull, CT 06611
(203) 452-1006
www.royalteacompany.net
Caters English tea parties for
special occasions.

Sundial Gardens & Tearoom
59 Hidden Lake Road
Higganum, CT 06441
(860) 345-4290
www.sundialgardens.com

T Salon & T Emporium
230 Fifth Avenue
New York, NY 10010
(212) 358-0506
www.tsalon.com

Tea & Sympathy
108 Greenwich Avenue
New York, NY 10011
(212) 989-9735
www.teaandsympathynewyork.com

Teaism
2009 R Street, NW
Washington, D.C. 20009
(877) 8TEAISM;
(202) 667-3827
www.teaism.com
Check Web site for additional locations.

Teany Café
90 Rivington Street
New York, NY 10002
(212) 475-9190
www.facebook.com/TeanyCafeOfficial.com

The Tearoom
7 East Broughton Street
Savannah, GA 31401
(912) 239-9690
www.savannahtearoom.com

The Tea Shoppe
26 Steeple Street
Mashpee Commons
Mashpee, MA 02649
(508) 477-7261

Thistlefields
36 N Howard Street
Gettysburg, PA 17325
(717) 338-9131

Tohono Chul Park Tearoom
7366 North Paseo Del Norte
Tucson, AZ 85704
(520) 742-6455
www.tohonochulpark.org

Windsor Court Hotel
300 Gravier Street
New Orleans, LA 70130
(888) 596-0955;
(504) 523-6000
www.windsorcourthotel.com

EUROPE & AUSTRALIA
Chewton Glen
New Milton, Hampshire
BH25 6QS, England
(800) 344-5087;
011-44-1425 27 5341
www.chewtonglen.com

Chez Angélina
226 Rue de Rivoli
75001 Paris
France
011-33-142-60-8200
www.angelina-paris.fr

The Four Seasons London
Hamilton Place, Park Lane
London W1J 7DR
England
011-44-207-499-0888
www.fourseasons.com/london

The Hotel Windsor
111 Spring Street
Melbourne, Victoria 3000
Australia
011-61-39-633-6000
www.thehotelwindsor.com.au

Kinnaird Estate
By Dunkeld
Perthshire PH8 0LB
Scotland
011-44-179-648-2440
www.kinnairdestate.com

Laduré
75 Avenue des Champs-Élysées
75008 Paris
France
011-33-140-75-0875
www.laduree.fr

The Ritz London
150 Piccadilly
London W1J 9BR
England
011-44-027-493-8181
www.ritzcarlton.com/hotels/london

Little London Café
35 Little London
Chichester, West Sussex PO19 PL
England
011-44-124-377-4900
www.littlelondoncafe.co.uk

Trinity House Tearoom
47 High Street
Manningtree, Essex
England C011 1AH
011-44-120-639-1410

The Willow Rooms
217 Sauchiehall Street
Glasgow G2 3EX
Scotland
011-44-141-332-0521
www.willowtearooms.co.uk
Visit Web site for address of other
location in Glasgow.

Tea Clubs, Organizations, and Museums

The Charleston Tea Plantation
6617 May Bank Highway
Wadmalaw Island, SC 29487
(843) 559-0383
www.charlestonteaplantation.com
Retail shop and tours organized
by Bigelow Tea.

Exclusive Journeys Over
A Cuppa Tea Tours
P.O. Box 759
Willimantic, CT 06226
(800) 467-1694;
(860) 423-2344
www.realadventures.com
Tea tours to Britain and Europe.

The Tea Association of the USA
362 Fifth Avenue, Suite 801
New York, NY 1001
(212) 986-9415
www.teausa.org

China National Tea Museum
Hangzhou, Zhjiang Province, China
english.teamuseum.cn

The Japanese Tea Garden
75 Hagiwara Tea Garden Drive
Golden Gate Park, San Francisco
(415) 752-1171
www.japaneseteagardensf.com

American Tea Masters Association
2782 Broadway, #302
San Diego, CA 92102
(619) 758-4101
www.teamasters.org

Recipe Index

Index

Photography Credits